WRITING COMMUNITY CHANGE

DESIGNING TECHNOLOGIES FOR CITIZEN ACTION

NEW DIMENSIONS IN COMPUTERS AND COMPOSITION

Gail E. Hawisher and Cynthia L. Selfe, editors

WRITING COMMUNITY CHANGE

CHANGE

DESIGNING TECHNOLOGIES FOR CITIZEN ACTION

Jeffrey T. Grabill
Michigan State University

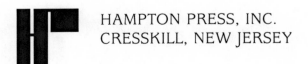

HAMPTON PRESS, INC.
CRESSKILL, NEW JERSEY

Printed in the United States of America

Library of Congress Cataloging-in-Publication Data

Grabill, Jeffrey T., 1968-
    Writing community change : designing technologies for citizen
    action / Jeffrey T. Grabill.
        p. cm. -- (New dimensions in computers and composition)
    Includes bibliographical references and index.
    ISBN 1-57273-762-X (hardbound) -- ISBN 1-57273-763-8 (pbk.)
  1. Communication in community development. 2. Communication in
  social action. 3. Community organization--Technological innovations.
  4. Authorship--Data processing. I. Title

  HN49.C6G73 2007
  307.1'402854--dc22

                                    2007006538

Hampton Press, Inc.
23 Broadway
Cresskill, NJ 07626

For Megan and Jackson

CONTENTS

5 Making Infrastructures to Support Invention 89

6 Writing Programs and Public Life 109

List of Figures

ACKNOWLEDGEMENTS

This is a book in which coordinated and collaborative work plays an important conceptual and practical role. This is true both for the work described in this book and for the work of the book itself. There are many, many people, machines, and institutions who (and that) made this book possible; indeed, who deserve to be called writers of this book.

In this book I report on a risk communication project in a place I call "Harbor." There are a group of people in Harbor working very hard to keep their community clean and their neighbors healthy. They have been good enough to let those of us working on that project to learn from them. They trusted us, let us into their homes and confidences, and in doing so, enabled this book and the more important work that we have done together. I hope we have done well by them so far. In any event, I owe them a considerable debt. If I learned anything from them, it is that I know how to repay that debt.

The work in Harbor was enabled by a group here at Michigan State University called Technical Outreach Services to Communities (TOSC). Tom Voice granted me access to their work, and Kirk Riley, my project manager, was always generous and supportive, even when he wasn't quite sure what we were really doing (those were the moments, of course, when he was most supportive).

Stuart Blythe is a special talent and colleague. After my first meeting with the TOSC folks here on my campus, I knew that we needed Stuart. He has a sharp and careful mind, a good heart, and is a fantastic listener. I am proud of what we have been able to do in Harbor so far, and that is due in large part to Stuart. Thank you, Stu.

In addition to the work in Harbor, this book reports on work that takes place here in the Lansing area. John Melcher of Michigan State University's

Community and Economic Development Program has been my mentor as I have attempted to learn about and from this community. He has enabled my access to a number of institutions, organizations, and conversations. Without John, the work we have done in Lansing is probably not possible. The Ingham County Public Health Department, which supports CACVoices, has also sponsored this work. Bruce Bragg, the Director of the Health Department, has consistently granted me access to the work of his department. In addition, our work in Lansing has been underwritten by a grant from Michigan State University's Office of Outreach and Engagement and by the Writing in Digital Environments Research Center at Michigan State. Hiram Fitzgerald, Associate Provost for University Outreach and Engagement, and Diane Zimmerman, Director, Center for the Study of University Engagement, were generous in allowing multiple readings of my research proposal and then funding it. The commitment to outreach research at Michigan State is serious and genuine.

Active collaborators in Lansing include LeRoy Harvey, a community member and long-time participant in local data democratization and capacity building projects; Marcus Cheatham, a Public Health Department statistician and leader of data democratization in the Lansing area; Sarah Swereinga, the Director of Michigan State University's Usability and Accessibility Center; and many individuals who have consented to work with us as participants and partners. I wish I could list you all.

It is important to thank Gail Hawisher and Cindy Selfe for their long-term support and for consistently publishing my work. Every time that I would share with them the feeling that I was working alone, they were always quick to make me feel as if I had company.

I am fortunate to work with fantastic colleagues. Doug Noverr, my chair, both understands what I do and why I do it. Everyone should be lucky enough to have such administrative and intellectual support. I am also fortunate to work with this rogue's gallery of talent: Damian Baca, David Cooper, Ellen Cushman, Dànielle DeVoss, Julie Lindquist, Malea Powell, Laura Julier, David Sheridan, Leonora Smith, Janet Swenson. Each has shaped my thinking and made coming to work fun. Thank you.

The Writing in Digital Environments Research Center has been both infrastructure and labor of love. It has been great fun to help build it, but it is also fundamental to my current work. Roberto Reyes and Ashley Kuhnmuench, both undergraduate professional writing majors, have participated in the research and writing of this book. Jim Ridolfo, Martine Rife, and Kendall Leon, three graduate assistants who have worked for the WIDE Center, have been good colleagues to me. Each has had a major impact on my work these past three years. Amy Diehl, my research assistant on the

CACI project, is truly special. She is sharp, careful, ethical, kind, and also a remarkable listener. Matt Penniman, who took over where Amy left off, is equally (and differently) talented and is ensuring, as a long-time Lansing resident, that we are good to the people with whom we are working. Jim Porter, a co-director of WIDE and a close colleague for many years, has helped make Michigan State a rich place to work. Bill Hart-Davidson has had perhaps the deepest impact on my thinking of late. Those who know Bill and his work will see it immediately. Bill has changed how I think about writing and writing technologies, and I enjoy working with him and learning from him.

My most essential collaborator by far is my partner Chandra. With her I am trying to write a life. In this effort she has been a patient and loving friend and a superior writer.

These collaborators and sponsors have given much to me. Thank you.

Permissions have been granted for the use of the following material:

Part of chapter 1 is a revision of text that appears in Jeffrey T. Grabill (2003) Community computing and citizen productivity. *Computers and Composition, 20*, 131-150. Used with permission of Elsevier Science.

1

WRITING TECHNOLOGIES AND COMMUNITY ACTION

The BBC has reported two stories that help explain what this book is about. Both concern the arctic. The first is about the Fabrication Labs that MIT is building around the world (Boyd, 2005). One reason for building these labs is an interest on the part of an MIT researcher in personal fabrication, the practice of ordinary people making technologies to solve local problems. The story reports on Haakon Karlsen, a sheep farmer, and his modification of a cell phone with GPS capabilities to track his sheep. Karlsen straps the phone on a sheep's collar, and when the phone sends a text message with the coordinates of its location, Karlsen can pinpoint the location of his sheep.

The second story reports on climate changes in the arctic (BBC World Service, 2001). Although the report includes scientific evidence for climate change from a number of studies, it also notes the importance of aboriginal knowledge in understanding climate change in the arctic. In the report, Rosemarie Kuptana, a resident of a Canadian arctic community and former president of the Inuit Circumpolar Conference, says this:

> Traditional Inuit knowledge about the world around us—like the weather, the animals, the migration patterns, the changes that we've seen—this is the knowledge that has been accumulated over many, many centuries. It's oral tradition: it's scientific knowledge. It's *our* scientific knowledge.

These two stories are connected by more than their location. They show two phenomena that are extremely important to this book and the rhetorical dynamics of people writing to change their communities. In both these stories, we see people making infrastructures to solve problems—technologies, tools, knowledge. We see people in communities inventing. We see the knowledge work of everyday life.

*   *   *

In a knowledge society, the work of citizenship is knowledge work.[1] Yet unlike the knowledge work in schools or corporate workplaces, the knowledge work of citizens is not well supported. Knowledge workers in business settings are commonly (or perhaps only ideally) supported by appropriate technologies, useful information, and helpful human collaborators; however, knowledge workers in communities often have little of this support.

When citizens fail to be persuasive, their shortcomings might not be due to skill, knowledge, imagination, philosophy, or organization. At least not precisely. The failure may be as simple, and as complex, as a failure to conceptualize and conduct work effectively. I argue that we—as researchers, teachers, citizens—have failed to understand rhetorical work in communities *as work*. This book attempts to understand the work of citizenship and imagine the support necessary for this work. I am interested principally in "writing," in the centrality of advanced information technologies to this writing work, and the design of civic infrastructures for community action.

*   *   *

For a few years now, I have been working on projects with people interested in effecting some change in their local communities. The work required of these people is complex. They must navigate institutions, learn to read expert "literatures," use advanced information technologies effectively, and write. Using current disciplinary terms, this work can be called "risk communication" or "computers and writing" or "literacy studies" or "professional and technical writing." Other academics with whom I have worked use their own disciplinary terms, such as "planning" or "civil engineering" or "community informatics."

I make two general types of arguments in this book, both based on my interest in how advanced information technologies are used to write (for) community change. The first is descriptive and asserts that the fields concerned with writing (rhetoric, composition, literacy studies) and writing technologies (computers and writing, technical and professional writing) have incomplete maps of what people actually do with writing and technologies in their day-to-day lives. The significant overlap between composition studies and computers and writing has provided rich descriptions of how students write with computers in schools, particularly in university classrooms. Technical and professional writing focuses on workplaces and school-to-work relationships. Rhetorical theory is interested in "the public."[2] Literacy theory, particularly since the New Literacy Studies, has generally been consciously unconcerned with the domain of work or deeply suspicious of the impact of workplace and market pressures on the meaning and practice of literacy (e.g., Brandt, 2001). This situation limits the analytical frames used to understand writing in communities. Specifically, it limits the ability to examine writing in community settings as highly complex, coordinated work that requires substantial infrastructure to be carried out effectively. To understand writing for community change in this way demands analytical insights and tools from all of the fields just mentioned.

The second type of argument I make in this book is about design. Here I focus on how to design information infrastructures that allow people to make things that matter to them and their communities. Both arguments are exercises in theory building, and I understand this theory to be a type of civic rhetoric for those who write with advanced information communication technologies (ICT) for community action—including our students—the civic rhetors of the 21st century.[3]

*   *   *

This book is an attempt to represent new (for me) methodological directions as well. At the heart of this book are two empirical studies of significant temporal scope. "Time," in this case, is part of that new direction, and it means something rather simple to me: The studies that form the core of this book are attempts to pay attention over time to how people are working in communities. The first study is a risk communication project in which we studied, in part, how citizens "did science" and communicated that science in an urban, heavily industrialized and polluted community called "Harbor." We have been paying attention to that community for three years now.[4] The second study examines the design and use of a community information resource in Lansing, Michigan. This project has ebbed and flowed over two years, and time, again, is the feature I wish to highlight. What we might think of as "longitudinal studies" are relatively rare in computers and writing and other, related fields. This impairs our ability to see change, understand impacts, and gauge both "success" and "failure." It limits what we can understand and how we build theory.

The second new direction is one for which I have imperfect language. "Applied" anthropologists think of it as "studying up" (e.g., van Willigen, Rylko-Bauer, & McElroy, 1989). Susan Leigh Star (1999), after Anselm Strauss, has called it "studying the unstudied," and Ralph Cintron (2002) thinks of it as studying the dragon—an examination of the operations of power, not merely the effects. Each source for this language is really concerned with a different dragon, but for me they provide a language for examining what I think is terribly important, namely, the infrastructure of possibility, or the mundane and often invisible discursive rules and practices that bound what we can do as writers and citizens.

Let me explain. In arguing that he has yet to see a true "critical ethnography," Cintron writes that ethnographic work fails to account for both vertical (institutional, bureaucratic) and horizontal (communal, social) dynamics embedded and operational in any site of study. Such an account is perhaps impossible to achieve in any one study, as Cintron notes, but he uses this claim to advance the idea that many ethnographers choose—because they have to choose something—subaltern, marginal, or vulnerable groups and thus study the effects of power. He wonders, therefore, if we fail to understand "the complexities of what it means to make social change . . . [change that is] typically the result of sly, subtle adjustments that somehow meet the needs of both the operations of power and the needs of the vulnerable" (pp. 940-941). It is an intriguing possibility.

My project is not of the type that Cintron imagines. I am not an ethnographer, and my work does not attempt the project of "critical ethnography." What I do represent in this book is one attempt at new understandings of the relationship between more (expert) and less (nonexpert) powerful actors (the horizontal axis), and an effort to pay attention to "boring things" (infrastructures, work, bureaucratic discourse—one way to think of the vertical axis). The methodological work described here is a major deliverable of the book. If we want to work effectively within communities, then we all need to understand more fully how institutions operate, how the powerful operate, and how infrastructures are designed and made. The "unstudied" in this case is not the margins, but the center. The body of the dragon.

A MUNDANE EXAMPLE OF WRITING

Nearly a decade ago now, Barbara Mirel (1996) wrote that "a major change is transforming the American workplace . . . [as] employees in every department can manage their own data and compose data reports for business purposes" (p. 91). She goes on to describe the use and importance of data reports for business organizations, asserting that the basic purpose of data reporting is to "support a reader's interpretive needs and strategies for turning that data into information and knowledge" (p. 92). In chapters 2 and 3, I return to what terms like "data," "information," and "knowledge" mean in contexts relevant to using ICTs to write for community change. What is important about Mirel's analysis is her understanding of the use of databases as a type of writing and her understanding of databases as thoroughly rhetorical.[5] The implications of these claims are significant. Mirel correctly notes that to understand writing in business organizations is to understand the relationships among problem solving, databases, and organizational writing itself. Furthermore, she suggests that the more one studies the complexity of user interactions with databases for writing, the more the line blurs between the databases themselves and the texts produced by using them. In other words, if the effective use of a database requires a deep, rhetorical knowledge of how databases are written, then the writing scene in business organizations, the very tools and resources for invention, include the database itself.

Mirel's claims might have been striking in 1996, but they are certainly not novel statements to make about business organizations—what we routinely call "knowledge organizations"—today. It is worth noting that Mirel's call for technical and professional writing to take up the study of databases has been largely ignored. Setting this aside, what is true for business organizations is just as true for community-based, neighborhood, cultural, and civic organizations today (and for some time now). Writing in communities and organizations entails the making and use of databases themselves. This is even more obviously true if one understands computer networks themselves as databases. Showing this claim to be true is my concern in chapter 4. But now let me provide an example to illustrate this claim.

Many people in the United States live in communities where one can access web-based databases in order to collect data relevant to public decision-making processes. Such information technology-driven initiatives, sometimes called "data democratization," are a common part of many economic development, planning, e-government, and activist programs. It is a significant example of a more widespread and commonplace view, driven by remarkable advances in ICTs over the last 20 years, that the information served by these technologies is, by itself, useful, and that people, by virtue of the fact that the information exists, make use of it in their day-to-day lives. In fact, the strongest statements about the power of information make an explicit connection between information and economic well being and, in so doing, mirror the even longer standing connections made between literacy and economic development (for critiques of this connection in literacy theory, see Goody, 1986; Graff 1979, 1988; Street 1984). The short version of the literacy-development narrative is that a certain level of literacy in a given economy, country, or region corresponds to a certain level of economic development, as if the latter were caused by the former.

There are a number of problems with these assumptions, of course. The most significant problem, in my view, is the invisibility of (the problem of) writing with computers enabled by a focus on "information" delivery. Consider the following interface from the birth records database, one of many databases in a community informatics website in Lansing, Michigan (see Fig. 1.1). A user accesses the birth records database two-to-three layers deep in the larger website. Once the user gets to this particular database, she is required to make complex technological and scientific choices, beginning with the meanings of terms, the choices of row or column variable as they pertain to this database and in terms of how they relate to each other, options regarding grouping tables, and choices to exclude missing variables. If our user plays with her options, the database returns a long table (see Fig. 1.2). If our user is like me, she is now completely lost. Devoid of context, what do the values mean? The layout and design are both problems. But more importantly, it isn't clear how this data can be used. Worse yet, the data might be misused because it is easy to overgeneralize or misapply it to situations.

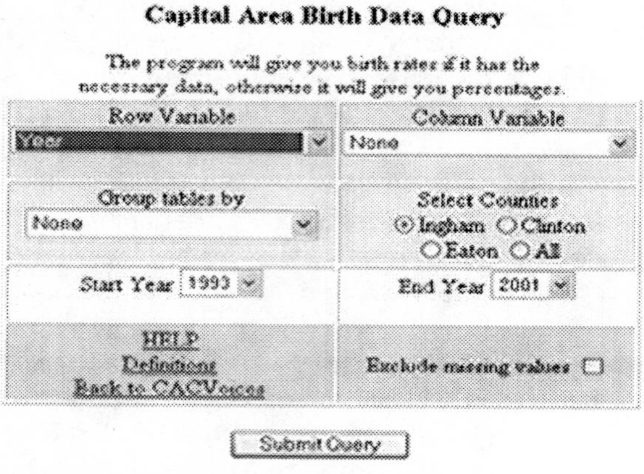

Capital Area Birth Data Query

The program will give you birth rates if it has the necessary data, otherwise it will give you percentages.

Row Variable	Column Variable
Year ▾	None ▾
Group tables by	Select Counties
None ▾	⊙ Ingham ○ Clinton ○ Eaton ○ All
Start Year 1993 ▾	End Year 2001 ▾
HELP Definitions Back to CACVoices	Exclude missing values ☐

Submit Query

Fig. 1.1 The main birth records database interface

What I have just described is a common, real moment of rhetorical invention and the very type of complex writing situation that Mirel describes as commonplace in the business organization of the late 1990s. It is more clear, I suppose, why employees in a corporate organization might need databases to write. But why would anyone "in the community" need to use this database? Related to that question, why are such databases even publicly accessible? One answer is that powerful tools such as a birth records database are available because they *can* be made available. Some organizations sponsor access out of a genuine desire to enable community capacity. Some sponsor such initiatives because they can become more efficient by "outsourcing" searching and interpretation to citizens themselves. Some organizations do it for both reasons. What is undeniably true is that powerful tools are available, and people use them because they provide access to powerful information that may be difficult to access in other ways. This is a good thing. If a community needs to make an argument for daycare, better prenatal care, or services and spaces based on population growth, a database like this is useful. Yet although computers and writing has been interested in helping students write with similar tools in schools, and technical and professional writing has been concerned with the workplace, we have largely missed the migration of knowledge work into communities. In short, there is little work available that might guide a neighborhood association, a group of students, an activist organization, or government employees trying to become more productive citizens.

This book is an attempt to fill that gap, not just because it is possible to fill or because there is clear disciplinary value in doing so (frankly, I am unsure of this—disciplines can function just fine in isolation), but because it is important to civic rhetorical practice and how we teach writing with computers in schools. Fundamentally, I am interested in what it means to be a "productive citizen" and the implications for supporting that productivity in a range of social institutions. Technology access is essential but insufficient. The ability to write effectively also matters, but one goal of this book is to change how we understand "writing," and so writing ability, as commonly understood, is only part of the answer as well. Rhetorical habits of mind—analytical skills, invention strategies, *kairos*—matter significantly, as do a number of other capacities, such as the ability to coordinate and manage work. Given all that, my point with this example is rather basic to stake out a claim that any attempt to understand writing for community action and change must account for the practices embedded in this example. Must understand the technologically mediated places where people invent new knowledge. Must understand that if citizens cannot access, assemble, and analyze the information they find, they will not be able to produce the necessary knowledge to participate in decision-making processes that affect their lives and communities.

UNDERSTANDING INFORMATION TECHNOLOGIES IN COMMUNITIES

I have been in conversation for some time now with a field called "community informatics" (e.g., Grabill, 2003a). I have been interested in this work because of its absence in rhetoric and composition and computers and writing (one notable exception in computers and writing: Regan & Zuern, 2000). That is, I have long been interested in community literacies and

Year by Trimester Care Began					
Frequency Row % Column %	First	Second	Third	Missing	Row Totals
1993	3186 78.55 10.45	598 14.74 21.79	108 2.66 19.64	164 4.04 15.69	4056 11.64
1994	3353 82.77 11.00	469 11.58 17.09	82 2.02 14.91	147 3.63 14.07	4051 11.63
1995	3336 86.51 10.94	318 8.25 11.59	39 1.01 7.09	163 4.23 15.60	3856 11.07
1996	3440 87.04 11.28	284 7.19 10.35	128 3.24 23.27	100 2.53 9.57	3952 11.35
1997	3600 90.25 11.81	245 6.14 8.93	27 0.68 4.91	117 2.93 11.20	3989 11.45
1998	3516 93.09 11.53	147 3.89 5.36	30 0.79 5.45	84 2.22 8.04	3777 10.84
1999	3413 92.95 11.19	143 3.89 5.21	22 0.60 4.00	94 2.56 9.00	3672 10.54
2000	3493 92.51 11.46	164 4.34 5.98	41 1.09 7.45	78 2.07 7.46	3776 10.84
2001	3155 85.22 10.35	376 10.16 13.70	73 1.97 13.27	98 2.65 9.38	3702 10.63
Column Totals	30492 87.54	2744 7.88	550 1.58	1045 3.00	34831

Fig. 1.2. Data table from birth records database

computers and writing, but people working in these two areas simply don't talk to each other. Yet one thing that has always struck me about my various experiences in community based institutions is the deep penetration of information technologies into people's everyday lives. Many of these interactions with information technologies, of course, require significant written literacies. The implications of the interactions between information technologies, writing, and public institutions mean that to study community literacies is to study things called *community computing, community networking*, or *community informatics*. Now, it is equally true that work in computers and writing is absent from the books and journals of those working in "community informatics," and so we have the unfortunately normal situation of closely related areas missing each other. This "gap" by itself isn't particularly important, interesting, or worth addressing. It is important to address only because without articulating these domains of inquiry, we will continue to see information technologies failing certain individuals and communities and persistent "divides" related to technology and writing.

So what is community informatics? Community informatics is often thought of as a parallel development to other domains of informatics work, such as management information systems (Gurstein, 2001, p. 265). It is also

> concerned with carving out a sphere and developing strategies for precisely those who are being excluded from this ongoing rush, and enabling these individuals and communities to take advantage of some of the opportunities which the technology is providing. It is also concerned with enhancing civil society and strengthening local communities for self-management and for environmental and economically sustainable development, ensuring that many who might otherwise be excluded are able to take advantage of the enormous opportunities the new technologies are presenting. (Gurstein, 2000, p. 2)

As scholars in this emerging field note, however, there is not a set of core questions, methodologies, and practices that are necessary for fuller development and definition (Denison, Johanson, Stillman, & Schander, 2003; Stoecker, 2005). At best, what community informatics *is not* may be most important. Community informatics is not principally about making new, bleeding edge information technologies themselves. It is not really engineering or mainstream computer science. And just as significantly in my view—and for this project—it is not principally about how individuals interact with machines and, thus, with designing machines to support individualized activity.[6] As I argue later in the book, the writing that I see in communities is either collaborative or cooperative, rarely individual in any meaningful sense. Thus, good community informatics strategies aim "to challenge the often well-intentioned but flawed policy initiatives to impose technological solutions to perceived social problems from above. Instead [community informatics] is an approach which stresses that technologies should be embedded within existing cultural and social relations" (Loader, Hague, & Eagle, 2000, p. 82). Despite the affordances of the work in community informatics, the field, perhaps surprisingly, does not orient itself to writing, and so, I would argue, it doesn't understand very well what people actually do with ICTs. This despite the fact that "productivity" has long been identified as a key problem area within community informatics.

The history of community computing projects repeatedly confronts issues related to citizen productivity. Anne Beamish (1995), who has written one of the few histories of community computing, describes community networks as providing community information and the means for community members to communicate, typically focusing on local issues, emphasizing access, and working toward social change or community development (for more history and background, see Schuler, 1996, 1997). This is why community networks have been called "intelligence systems for local communities" (Ars Portalis, 2000, p. 2), and why so much money has been spent to prove this true: cities investing in electronic town halls; planning departments using networks for planning activities and in some cases creating neighborhood websites and databases; and neighborhood and civic organizations creating neighborhood information infrastructures.

Community informatics projects are not uncommon, although their success and failure is often measured using rough and immediate measures of access. As I discuss in chapters 2 and 3 in particular, many of these initiatives are concerned with information access, which is both useful and troubling as a measure of possibility. As is often pointed out, somebody owns the physical infrastructure used to create community networks, and that ownership is obviously meaningful because of its policy and maintenance implications. Those who own the infrastructure determine to varying degrees what happens with it. Depending on the interpretation of intellectual property policies and laws, those who own the network also own the information on that network.[7] The high costs of public ownership of computer networks means that many network access points are either privately or jointly owned because freenets and other such systems, with some exceptions, lack the capital to keep pace with technological and market-driven changes. And the telecommunications industry is currently pushing legislation through states in the United States to limit publicly owned ISPs and networks. The profit motive doesn't always fit well with the traditional community networking goals of community development or greater social justice. Thus, what an Ars Portalis (2000) white paper calls "the Faustian bargain of the digital divide" often emerges: "past funding policies and priorities have shifted from encouraging community networks to be 'public access internet on-ramps' to become electronic 'one-stop-shops' for social services" or commerce-driven spaces that encourage consumer behavior (p. 5).

The complexities of building, maintaining, and using community networks suggest reasons why advocates are concerned about "productivity." Productivity is what computers and writing would understand as "writing" or "composing," and what I also call at various places "making" or "performance." Anne Beamish (1999) speculates that the community computing movement could be in trouble "because . . . participants are frequently seen as passive consumers of information rather than active producers. Information is emphasized rather than the communicative side of the technology. And perhaps worst of all, projects too often view the technology as an end in itself rather than a means to an end" (p. 351). ICTs are too often narrowly articulated as information devices. According to this way of thinking, information is why people use computers and networks; information is by itself useful; and information is the solution to a host of economic and social problems. However, information by itself isn't particularly useful; people need to be taught how to use information (in addition to learning how to assemble and make sense of massive amounts of information). On balance, having more information certainly seems better than having less. Furthermore, a strong case can be made that the most expedient value of advanced information technologies, particularly for distressed communities, is the information it allows users to access. Yet this same view of information and the tools used to gather it articulates information technologies in ways that limit the usefulness of "information" and the activities of the people who use it.

What clearly emerges from this discussion is a much more complex set of questions related to access and digital divides, issues the field of computers and writing has addressed for many years. In terms of the broad demographic categories historically used by the Federal government to measure access, the divide is still highly correlated to income, education, and race/ethnicity. This means that the divide between rich and poor, white and nonwhite, highly educated and not continues to exist. And because it continues to exist, it continues to describe situations of social hierarchy and inequality that are harmful. But this demographic understanding of digital divides, although important, reveals very little. What we miss when we focus on the statistics is that access is a moving target with horizontal and vertical vectors (as Cintron might suggest).

Howard Besser (2001), for example, calls our attention to other critical gaps. These gaps include knowing how to use ICTs, knowing how to
understand and use the massive amounts of information available, and
knowing how to be productive with ICTs. Besser writes,

> in a digital age we need to teach our students how to author and dis-
> tribute digital works. . . . Those with this kind of access will be able to
> explore their creativity and gain experience in becoming content pro-
> ducers (not just consumers of works that others have produced). This
> also has direct application to the ability of underserved communities to
> produce information about their own communities. The digital divide
> also includes a gap between those who can be active creators and dis-
> tributors of information, and those who can only be consumers.
> (unpaginated)

Besser's claim is not only true for students in classrooms. It is equally true
for citizens acting in and through neighborhood and civic organizations,
grandparents and kids working and learning at a community media center,
or for me and my neighbors working to create persuasive plans for traffic
flow patterns around our community. Yet as Besser also notes, "[m]ost digital divide efforts have been aimed at enlarging the pool of receptive users
of content. . . . The thrust of these initiatives has been to create a new body
of digital age consumers." One way through this mess for those working in
community informatics is Gurstein's (2003) concept of "effective use."
Gurstein argues that policy remedies for the digital divide have been fixed
on technical solutions to human use problems. He insists—as do I—that
the critical issue with respect to the social impact of information technologies is the extent to which nonexpert, nontraditional users of technologies,
especially those typically marginalized, can become productive with
advanced information technologies in a way that expands local capacity to
achieve citizen objectives. This imperative—productivity with advanced
ICTs to achieve local goals—is at the heart of "effective use" and a worthy
goal for designing ICTs to support community action. Community informatics work at its best, then, is the study of how advanced ICTs are embedded in existing community, cultural, and social relations to enable people
to work effectively. Because advanced ICTs often aren't embedded or
enabling, community informatics at its best has a design imperative to
make new infrastructures with communities.

COMMUNITY ACTION

It is commonplace to think that citizens often have very little say and almost no power to effect public policy, even when it affects their own neighborhood. Frank Fischer (2000) asserts that "despite the contemporary emphasis on citizenship, democratic theorists largely remain distant from the level of citizen . . . such theorists mainly labor at the abstract level of nation-state and, in doing so, neglect the everyday aspects of deliberative politics, especially as they relate to ordinary people" (p. xi). This is largely true, yet as one of those political theorists correctly observes, ordinary people are often inhibited from participating in decisions that affect their lives because they lack the "technical expertise, authority . . . and status" needed to participate directly in those decisions (Young, 2000, pp. 56-57). Clearly, such participation requires that citizens also have an understanding of complex issues in order to articulate their experiences and participate in the discussion. Citizens armed with both an understanding of the issues, as well as the local knowledge of how those issues will affect their community, can offer very valuable contributions to any decision. But the requirements for ethical and effective public deliberation must confront a set of what Asen (2002) calls "indirect exclusions."[8] Indirect exclusions "function tacitly through discursive norms and practices that prescribe particular ways of interacting in public forums" (p. 345). The significant body of literature on public deliberation and discourse ethics is one response to indirect exclusions, and although important for the models and rules developed for conceptualizing a deliberative public sphere and promoting ethical communication, they don't help us deal with forums in which indirect exclusions are built into the nature of the system and process. They don't help us understand, in other words, how to act in most public forums. They do not deal effectively with problems of knowledge or invention, or what Dahlgren (2000) calls the "relevant knowledge and competency" condition of civic culture:

> People must have access to reliable reports, portrayals, analyses, discussions, debates, and so forth about current affairs. . . . Accessibility has to do not just with technical and economic aspects but also with linguistic and cultural proximity. The sources of knowledge and the materials for the development of competencies must be comprehensible, cast in modes that communicate well with different collectivities. . . . They also must have the ability to express their own ideas if they are to partake in the public sphere's processes of opinion formation and/or engage in

need to new
civic rhetoric

other political activities; communicative competencies are indispensable for a democratic citizenry. Education, in its many forms, will thus always retain its relevance. (p. 337)

What is clearly relevant is the need for a new type of civic rhetoric that enables one to work through various indirect exclusions.

This rhetoric has two broad, interpenetrating "canons," one dealing with invention, the other with performances because there are two fundamental problems facing "nonexpert" participants in public deliberations— a problem of knowledge and a problem of performance.[9] Both problems require the use of ICTs for "writing." Indeed, the use of these technologies to perform is part of the problem. Consider the fact that citizen participants at a public meeting are often characterized (by government officials, industry representatives, and university researchers) as people who know nothing and who rant emotionally about irrelevant issues.[10] The fact is, however, that nonexpert citizens can be effective, but in order to be effective, they must have an Art that is powerfully inventive and performative.

To talk about invention is to revisit a concept that has become increasingly invisible in the larger field of rhetoric and composition and has never been an explicit focus in computers and writing.[11] In fact, the visibility of invention has been cyclical throughout the history of rhetoric (see, e.g., Bryant, 1965; Lauer, 2004). As we learn from Lauer (2004), invention disappears, at least in part, because the social and historical moments of its demise do not question issues of truth or knowledge. So, for example, if all truth comes from God, and if that truth is present in known places (the Book), then what is needed is hermeneutics, not heuristics. If "knowledge" is believed only to come from "science," then the usefulness of rhetoric is the effective arrangement of knowledge developed by science (or philosophy, depending on the historical moment).

When citizens find themselves in a situation in which they must challenge a powerful understanding of who they are, what they are capable of, or the utility and value of the physical space they inhabit, they find themselves at a moment that is ambivalently rhetorical. They find themselves, that is, confronting audiences that understand knowledge to be produced by individuals and organizations of expertise, but who do not understand the production of knowledge to entail rhetoric. At the same time, they confront exigencies that demand new knowledge production on their part in order to tell an alternative story about identity, capability, and place. This alternative epistemological process is understood to entail rhetoric to the extent that it is characterized as something other than institutionalized expertise—something such as narrative or anecdote, or as emotional or

use narrative

interested. Thus, rhetoric exists in an uneasy tension with science, just as citizens and communities exist in an uneasy tension with expert institutions. The rhetorical ambivalence of this situation becomes explicit when these forms of knowledge converge. What is almost always true is that the "alternative" rhetorical moves of the less powerful are understood as "politics" or "activism" or "NIMBYism" or "railroading," and as many other things. Not science or truth. What most discussions of this dynamic fail to appreciate is the deeply rhetorical nature of these civic moments (see Fischer, 2000). That is, that the very conflict itself *is* civic rhetoric. Further, the precise inventional practices of citizens, and increasingly the role of advanced information technologies in these practices, are often missed because the default assumption is that "nonexperts" in communities don't "do" science or technology. Such an assumption is supported, of course, by the belief that the processes of science are separate from those of rhetoric.[12] As Miller (1985) writes, it is only recently that it was even possible to speak of invention in relation to technical and scientific discourse: "In classical treatments of rhetoric, scientific discourse was excluded because its end was seen as very different from that of rhetoric: science concerns the certain, the demonstrably true, whereas rhetoric concerns the probable, matters of opinion" (pp. 116-117). But as Lauer (2004) points out, with the rise of the new rhetoric in the middle of the 20th century, rhetoric and invention became increasingly important as philosophy and the social sciences continually confronted situations of uncertainty, probability, and deeply situated and nuanced issues of epistemology, ideology, and value. Thus, to study how citizens become persuasive to support community change is necessarily to study expertise and science and technology and view them through a rhetorical lens.

The theory that I build in this book—a theory concerned with how people write with ICTs for community change—is a rhetoric. It is concerned with "studying up" or examining the practices of the powerful. At the same time, it is built from the ground up, from how people in communities already do the knowledge work of citizenship. This is a rhetoric concerned with the day-to-day rhetorical practices of "everyday people." Here the teachers are communities, organizations, and individuals who engage in rhetorical practices, with varying degrees of success, in nearly every community. What inventional strategies are effective? Why? How do we know them to be effective? And can we draw from these a *techne* that can be taught to others? Because the answers to these questions are so important, the rhetoric I imagine is genuinely relevant to writing instruction in schools. Are our writing programs concerned with producing thoughtful and effective citizens? If so, then this book suggests how they must write as citizens. Effective performances in communities are embodied in meeting notes and agendas, flyers and newsletters, websites and iMovies, meetings and protests, letters and reports. It is obvious that a meaningful civic rhetoric that is effective in contemporary public spaces must help people write, speak, and compose new media effectively. They must perform persuasively. What may not be obvious is the nature of these performances. These are not the sorts of "great speeches" that are often analyzed in rhetoric scholarship. These performances are mundane documents, "emotional" rants delivered while standing on folding chairs, and pictures of drug sales on street corners.

A couple of years ago now, right after a community meeting that I attended as part of the risk communication project that I describe in this book, I overheard a woman remark to a friend, "we may be poor, but we aren't stupid." I have since come to know this woman and her organization, and she and her colleagues are anything but stupid. They have the rhetoric that I want to understand. This rhetoric articulates technological and institutional infrastructures, scientific and rhetorical expertise, nonexpert ways of knowing and expression, and public decision-making processes. Rhetoric is no longer the terrain of the individual rhetor speaking or writing to "the public." Although I realize that this subject position has not been the default for some time, this rhetoric *requires* collaboration of a breadth and depth perhaps not seen before (or made visible in previous scholarship). The design of information technologies to enable effective use is not something that "everyday people" can do by themselves, nor is it possible for designers and scientists working on their own. The writing practices of citizens engaged in community action requires the collaboration of large numbers of people (and tools and infrastructures). No document is singly authored, no speech a solo performance, no organization outside a complex institutional infrastructure. Rhetoric has always enabled this type of productivity, and indeed, as Janet Atwill (1998) has argued, the art's purpose is to enable the transgressive acts of the least powerful. The value of any contemporary art of rhetoric will be measured as it always has been—by how useful it (and we) can be for others.

NOTES

1.   Knowledge work is typically understood as "analytical" and thus requiring problem solving and abstract reasoning, particularly with (and through)

advanced information technologies. Johnson-Eilola (2005) notes that knowledge work is also typically concerned with the production of information, as distinct from the production of material goods, and he also usefully points out that increasing numbers of us don't just work with information, we inhabit it. Thus, knowledge work, or what Johnson-Eilola calls *symbolic production*, is the making of largely discursive performances that, quite literally, do work (pp. 3-4).

2. Many contemporary discussions of civic rhetoric focus on structured political, legal, or ceremonial events. These discussions of civic rhetoric focus on how particular groups construct activist discourse, such as the civic practices of women (see Eldred & Mortensen, 1998); or the social justice rhetoric in African American sermons, slave narratives, and African American jeremiad (see Gilyard, 1999); or on the analysis of public speeches and the construction of various publics (Asen & Brouwer, 2001; Warner, 2002).

3. I use the convention "information communication technologies" (ICTs) throughout the book for the following reasons: (a) it better describes the articulation of computer and communications technologies like computers, networks, cell phones, and PDAs; and (b) it is consistent with work outside computers and composition (e.g., social informatics) and in other contexts (e.g., Europe) and therefore is one way to knit together work from these different contexts.

4. The "we" here includes my colleagues in Technical Outreach Services to Communities (TOSC), particularly Kirk Riley. TOSC is an outreach program located in civil and environmental engineering at Michigan State University. TOSC is funded by an EPA Hazardous Substance Research Centers grant. Stuart Blythe has been my collaborator on this work, as have a handful of individuals in this community. Other parts of this chapter have been written with my colleague Michele Simmons and have been enabled by other individuals, institutions, and technologies. This type of distributed inventional activity, collaborative and coordinated work, and network of support is not just normal, it is necessary. It is what knowledge work looks like.

5. As Mirel notes, the first study of this kind is Patricia Sullivan's (1986) dissertation on the use of electronic search systems in libraries. Sullivan's work was some of the earliest on electronic "card catalogs," an early, and perhaps first, connection between databases and writing, and almost certainly the first work to understand databases and their use as rhetorical.

6. Think here of usability, which I discuss later in the book. I teach and conduct usability inquiries and find the results useful. However, there is a danger in falling in love with usability, and this love affair is particularly strong in technical and professional writing right now. Usability can tell us a great deal about how an individual interacts with a computer interface; it cannot tell us much about use over time, and, most importantly, it is a poor way to capture collaborative or cooperative work.

7. Intellectual property is emerging as a key site of struggle for those interested in public space and democratic practice—in writing itself. IP issues are fundamental once we are involved with people in communities making things they would like to share and reuse over computer networks.

8. Direct exclusions are less interesting but obviously important. When a decision-making body or process is closed down to others as a function of naked political power, or when the explicit purpose of a process is only to inform citizens of decisions already made, then much of what I discuss here is irrelevant. Of course, in these situations, rhetoric is irrelevant as well.

9. Let me be clear regarding my use of the concept "nonexpert." I mean it largely as a shorthand, along with the concept of "expert," for relations of power operating in all civic forums and institutions. In chapters 4 and 5, I articulate an alternative epistemological value system that makes clear the high value I place on "nonexpert" ways of knowing.

10. The characterization of citizens as "emotional" is commonplace in the risk assessment and communication literature (see Fischoff, Watson, & Hope, 1984; Rowan, 1994a, 1994b; Sandman, 1990; Slovic, 1986). I have witnessed and overheard characterizations of this kind numerous times and, frankly, have seen some pretty dismal performances by citizens (and equally dismal performances by "experts").

11. I find discussions of the development of writing software in the early years of computers and writing to be perhaps the most interesting moments in the field in terms of thinking about and supporting invention.

12. It is true that work in the rhetoric and philosophy of science and technology, as well as work in the "rhetoric of inquiry" movement, have challenged these long-held views and assumptions. The perspectives that come from this intellectual work have not penetrated far beyond the academy, however.

2

UNDERSTANDING CIVIC INFORMATION AND INFRASTRUCTURES

I sit and puzzle through the differences between information and knowledge. At breakfast. The back of my toasted oats box asks me, "Do you have information or knowledge?" And then it tells me, "Information is a fact about a specific thing. Knowledge is when you have both information and understanding because of your experience." Problem solved. No need to pursue research that can be answered by my cereal box. I continue, however, not so much because the answer on the box is too simple but because it is there at all. We are so awash in information (as the cliché goes) that even children need to know the difference between knowledge and information. At breakfast.

I continue with my inquiry into what "information," "data," and "knowledge" might be, for despite the fact that my kids might have a solid grasp of these concepts, I don't. Not only that, but in my time observing and working with community computing projects, following various conversations about information communication technologies (ICTs), and teaching technical communication—which concerns itself with information design and architecture—I have seen few examinations of these concepts. So perhaps the makers of my cereal are on to something. Perhaps the concepts are so important that kids and their sleepy parents need a primer in the morning. Perhaps notions of information and knowledge and how they might play out in our day-to-day lives are already deeply embedded—deep enough to be part of the packaging of consumer products.

Why are these concepts so important? One reason that I suggest in this chapter is that "information" has deep cultural meaning arising at a particular time and place, capturing both popular imagination and policy-making as well. Thus, we have an information economy, an information society, an idea that the political economy can be organized around the production of information, and pervasive uses of information communication technologies in our lives. To my knowledge, this cultural-economic history has not been written, and although the dynamic to which I allude here is one reason to focus on the concept of information, it is not, in the end, why these concepts are so important to writing in community contexts. Rather, these concepts are important for less dramatic reasons, namely, the fact that if the work of citizenship is knowledge work, then this work must be supported by appropriate tools and resources. At this moment, these tools and resources are understood to be "information" technologies and systems. I argue in this book that "information infrastructures" frame what is possible for writers and writing in community contexts; therefore, interventions at the level of infrastructure are necessary to enable citizen action in communities. As I argue in this chapter, however, to get to the point of intervention—indeed, in order to understand the work I present later in this book—it is first necessary to unpack how information means and where it comes from. There exists a strong cultural narrative arguing that access to information is the key to a host of social goods. Whether or not this is true depends on situated, cultural, rhetorical, and infrastructural issues. It depends as well on what one means by "information" and its relationship to similar and, in some cases, much more powerful concepts like "data" and "knowledge."

DATA / INFORMATION / KNOWLEDGE

There is great power in contemporary notions of information. Since the development of information communication technologies (ICTs), their relatively widespread distribution in the workplaces, schools, and homes of the "developed world," and the creation of whole industries and economies to produce, distribute, and consume information, information has become a powerful social good. It is and probably always will be a good thing to have more and better information than to have less and worse information. Access to good information is bedrock to theories of capitalism and a contested commodity in market practices. Histories of diplomacy and stories of espionage concern themselves with who knows what, when, why, how, and if what is known is "true." Information has in some sense always animated theories of library design and the values associated with public and private libraries of all types. Much more recently, strategies devised to combat digital divides have centered on access to information.

Therefore, rather strong statements about the power of information exist, and perhaps the most pervasive and powerful of these statements concerns the connection between information and economic well-being. As I suggested in the first chapter, there is a long history of linking literacy to economic development.[1] Similarly, John Feather (1998) writes that "The relationship between information and development appears to be close" (p. 121), citing a number of newly industrialized Asian countries as examples of the connection between development and a sophisticated information technology infrastructure (for more complicated views on the same theme, see Corey, 2000; Rimmer, 2000; and especially Gibbs, Tanner, & Walker, 2000). To a degree, the claim that access to information and information technology drives development is most certainly true.[2] Information access and specialized knowledge are critical to any number of economic enterprises, but it doesn't necessarily follow as a matter of policy on international, national, or local levels that access to information and information technology will drive, create, or allow economic development (see Schön, Sanyal, & Mitchell, 1999, especially Sanyal & Schön, 1999). In fact, the reverse may be true. A certain level of existing economic activity makes possible and establishes a need for ICT development.

My point is simply to note the various ways that power and agency have been given to "information" in various macro contexts, and to note as well that this is a particularly powerful narrative within an information or knowledge economy. I am suggesting as well that such a narrative is relevant to the work of citizens. It is true that information cannot be an agent—people, organizations, and institutions have agency. It is also clear that there is no shared notion of what "information" actually means (or perhaps more accurately, *how* it means), which makes stories about the power of information difficult to follow. I can never get a handle on the main character.

So what is meant by information? Given the power attached to it, one would think that definitions and discussions would be plentiful. Definitional discussions are not plentiful, except perhaps on cereal boxes. There are some disciplines that do tackle the issue, library and information science being the most visible. And there is also management, economics, political science, and the rare salvo from the humanities using "information" and often the computer as a name for all that is wrong in the world (e.g., Bousquet, 2003; Liu, 2004; Wurman, 1989, offers the best take on the impact of the information economy on the humanities).

In fact, there is quite a long line of thinking about information. As Venturelli (forthcoming) shows, philosophers have long puzzled the relationships among information, knowledge and what we would now call "development," although the language used is quite different from the language deployed by economists today. More recently, the centrality of information in systems theory—indeed, the development of systems theory itself—has played a powerful role in the centrality of the term in contemporary life. It is easy to trace systems theory to the work on "cybernetics" by Wiener (1948, 1950), but work on systems theory/cybernetics exploded across the social and natural sciences after World War II (e.g., Simon, 1969). For communication studies, perhaps no instance of the systems theory revolution has been more important and persistent than Shannon and Weaver's (1964) largely unintended impact on human communication theory.

This audience may be well aware of Shannon and Weaver's linear communication model, which described communication as a flow of information from a source to a destination. Intended originally as a description of telecommunication transmissions, it quickly was used to describe human communication, a use that persists despite the many critiques of the model in various scholarly literatures. Linear and efficient models of communication, such as the Shannon-Weaver model, persist as an elegant description of human communication, largely because of their predictive power. Shannon and Weaver provided a theory that could be tested and refined, and so their work supported the methods of normative social (communication) science. It enabled science to get done, and so it was useful to science, if not communicative practice itself. But what is most interesting to me about this work is, in fact, its persistence. It is still commonplace to see modifications of the Shannon and Weaver model of communication—if not the original—in textbooks and scholarly work. My speculation that the theory has enabled years of normative communication science is insufficient to explain the model's persistence. The strength of Shannon and Weaver's theory is that it reinforces deep and widespread beliefs about the relationships between technology and communication. Communication *still* is often thought of as passing information across a network, even by those who talk about a "networked society" or an "information society" or by those who fundamentally understand communication as networked. In other words, our communication theory has not caught up with our social and cultural theory, and so when scholars and policymakers consider how best to design and leverage advanced information technologies in communities (or even to support knowledge work in organizations), they default to a thin notion of the relationships among human beings, technology, and communication that has not advanced much since the middle of the 20th century. Consider the recent work in "knowledge management" as it relates to concepts like data, information, knowledge, and communication.[3]

Davenport and Prusak (1998), writing about knowledge management within business organizations, parse their terms in this way. Data is "a set of discrete, objective facts about events" (p. 2). Examples include records, transactions, and other bits that by themselves mean very little. Data is the raw material of the knowledge organization. Information is a message, "usually in the form of a document or an audible or visible communication . . . it has a sender and a receiver . . . [and] is meant to change the way the receiver perceives something, to have an impact on his judgment and behavior" (p. 3). Knowledge, they write, "is broader, deeper, and richer than data or information" (p. 5). Knowledge is

> a fluid mix of framed experience, values, contextual information, and expert insight that provides a framework for evaluating and incorporating new experiences and information. It originates and is applied in the minds of knowers. In organizations, it often becomes embedded not only in documents or repositories but also in organizational routines, processes, practices, and norms. (p. 5)

For Davenport and Prusak, then, the differences among data, information, and knowledge are "a matter of degree" (p. 1). The concepts overlap significantly but are not interchangeable.

Like Davenport and Prusak, Brown and Duguid (2000) are similarly interested in the relationships among the three terms. Unlike Davenport and Prusak, they think knowledge management is a fad, and they take a more critical and nuanced stance regarding the relationships among information, communication, and organizational life, a stance I agree with. Brown and Duguid question if data leads to information and then to knowledge. They wonder as well if data can be aggregated into knowledge, or similarly, if knowledge can be disaggregated into data. Brown and Duguid are ultimately resisting a number of pressures at the same time. They critique futurists and information enthusiasts (most particularly knowledge management gurus) for dismissing processes and technologies (like paper) because such a dismissal ignores human needs (see Sellen & Harper, 2001, for more on the importance of paper). They dismiss information enthusiasts for prescribing more information as the solution to our problems—most ironically as a solution to the problem of having too much information. What they do assert, however, is the primacy of human networks in distinguishing that which is useful and that which isn't. Therefore, when it comes to notions of "information" and "knowledge," Brown and Duguid believe that information can be detached from human activity. It exists as an independent object. However, they insist that knowledge requires human activity, is difficult to "detach" from humans, and most importantly, is a function of learning. Learning is a highly complex phenomenon not easily understood and shared. And even for Brown and Duguid, information itself isn't completely discrete. They write that "[f]or all information's independence and extent, it is people, in their communities, organizations, and institutions, who ultimately decide what it all means and why it matters" (p. 18).

Despite the ambivalence of people like Brown and Duguid, a good number of people and institutions *have* decided that information's independence and power means that it is a valued commercial good—a commodity—and therefore a significant number of attempts to define information focus on this issue. Philip Agre (1995), for example, writing to librarians, notes four assumptions about the meaning of information, assumptions that he doesn't agree with (p. 225):

- It is a "thing," what he calls a "mass noun like 'milk,' 'flour,' and 'money'"
- It is a substance that can be distributed and commodified
- It is a content "divorced from any specific realization"
- It is neutral

Librarians and information scientists like Agre, who have watched the transformation of libraries and intellectual property law, understand the implications of a definition of information as a discrete "thing" that can be produced, distributed, and consumed (see Mosco & Wasko, 1988). Dan Schiller (1988) explores information as a "thing" in terms of why, when, and how information became defined (and valued) in such a way that it became a commodity. That is, he explores the source of its "detachment." He writes

> Why was not the status of information a major topic of information theory in 1700, 1800, or 1900? Why was it only in the postwar period that the economic role and value of information took on such palpable importance? With such questions the advocates of information's innately distinctive economic role are, of necessity, unconcerned. They find it difficult to explain the history of their own subject without retreating into technological determinism: the "computer revolution" becomes responsible for the unprecedented visibility and economic

significance of information. But this is no answer. For why was there a "computer revolution"? Why only in the postwar era? Why predominately in the developed market economies? And what kind of upheaval did this "revolution" actually portend? (p. 32)

Schiller's questions are useful, at the very least because they refuse to allow effects to be confused with causes, which is critical to the operation of any information mythology. Such myths insist that the power and value of information is the cause of a given change or social good, not the result of deeper or prior processes. Schiller's point is to refute the argument that information is a "resource" or a commodity of a different order from others, and, therefore, the argument for an economy and social order outside of historical labor processes. Schiller's method is to distinguish between a "resource," which is something of "actual or potential use" and a "commodity," which "bears the stamp of society and of history in its very core" (p. 33). For Schiller, information is a commodity subject to the same historical and social processes of other commodities. The differences between someone like Schiller and knowledge management advocates like Davenport and Prusak are those of history and ideology, and these differences are significant. Thinkers like Davenport and Prusak would have us understand our current moment as a break with history, driven by new social relations between and among information, technologies, organizations, and human beings. Not so with people like Schiller, nor, in different ways, with Agre, Brown, and Duguid. They would have us understand our current moment as historically situated and not precisely "new." There is a striking similarity, however, in nearly everyone's acceptance of the idea of information as a commodity: to be produced, distributed, and consumed like other commodities; subject to laws of trade, commerce, and property just like other commodities; subject to the "laws" of scarcity, supply, and demand just like other commodities; and like any commodity, once "consumed," able to fulfill a need.

Although the idea of information as a commodity is powerful and commonplace, it is insufficient because it assumes use; that is, it assumes that information is usable and useful. Such an assumption is part of the violence of any information myth, as I show later. This assumption of use also erases alternative notions of information and knowledge that do speak to use and that complicate, in significant ways, the notion that information is a "thing."

Although it may or may not be accurate or useful to think of "information" as a commodity, those concerned with what information is and how it means seem to agree that it sits somewhere in a linear model of development. But what if this isn't true? What if the meaning and value of infor-mation and knowledge is situated within a project team, a classroom, an organization, or a discipline? This is the point that Philip Agre (1995) makes. In challenging his earlier list of the four assumptions of informa-tion, he writes:

> [i]nformation is not a natural category whose history we can extrapo-late. Instead information is an element of certain professional ideolo-gies, most particularly librarianship and computing, and cannot be understood except through the practices within which it is constructed by the members of those professions and their work. (p. 225)

In other words, what we call "information" and what that means to us depends on contexts and institutions like disciplines and professional com-munities. Only then is it possible to understand what "information" is and can mean. Agre continues:

> library patrons may or may not conceive of themselves as looking for "information." Academic research professions, for example, orient not to "information" but to "literatures." Most literatures are associated with keywords such as "organizations," "activity," "networks," or "plan-ning," though these words might be employed in wholly different ways by unrelated disciplinary communities. Of course, librarians are well aware of the significance of these words to their users, and of the con-sequences of their choices of indexes (Fidel 1994). But a literature is more than that. It has a history (founders, milestones, rise and fall) and a structure (founding texts, survey articles, textbooks). Each of these in turn reflects a set of practices (research methods, standards of evi-dence, forms of argument) and a system of institutional relationships (dominant and dissident lines of thought, powerful and marginal research groups, politics of publication and funding). A research com-munity's insiders read its literature with these things in mind; indeed, these larger forces shape the specific genres of writing and the proto-cols of reading in which the community's members are skilled (Bazerman 1988). Threading one's way through the archives to recon-struct a literature is a rite of passage for research people entering a new field, and standard reference works offer only limited assistance with the process. A bibliography might map certain regions of a literature, but most often with a degree of "flatness" that does not nearly map the complex and differentiated terrain which the researcher experiences. (p. 226)

Agre argues that the largely linear models that I have glossed here regarding the relationships among data, information, and knowledge are all wrong. Although many people may think of knowledge creation as a process that begins first or even simply with collecting "information," Agre provides some important qualifications. Of course, people go to the library looking for something—and libraries increasingly see themselves as information resources—but in calling what a library contains something other than "information," Agre first acknowledges that information is already shaped. In other words, a discrete information "thing" is neither discrete nor "merely" information. It is most likely an artifact, to be sure, but it is purposeful, linked, and interconnected, and part of a web of other resources. More important, perhaps, is what it takes to understand a literature. Agre correctly notes that learning to understand a literature is a rite of passage in many academic disciplines that involves searching, judgment, reading practices, disciplinary history and understanding, and the ability to understand and create standard genres. All are productive acts. All are acts that require others and involve institutionally and/or communally situated learning.

My purpose here has been to demystify the concept of *information* by calling attention to its instability as a concept and the unreflective way in which agency has been attached to it. The instability is reinforced by calling attention to the fluid relationships among concepts like "data," "information," and "knowledge." The question that interests me is how we should understand "information" and the pragmatic potential of information communication technologies to enable people to achieve immediate personal and communal goals. That is, if we believe that the meaning and value of information (and knowledge) is situated in human and technical systems, structures, and activities, and if we begin to move away from the commonplace notion that information is a "thing" produced somewhere in a linear (production) process, then we might move toward a way of more fully understanding information as imbricated in larger and deeper infrastructures. It is these infrastructures that constitute major supports for writing in communities. These infrastructures also constitute the major impediments to effective writing in communities.

INFRASTRUCTURE

There is a deeper sense in which one can begin to understand "information," and it is a meaning hinted at by information theorists interested in

knowledge management within business contexts. The business management literature is fixated on systems as a solution to an organization's
information problems. Thus, knowledge management practice within business organizations is often seen as a function of servers, networks, and
databases. This approach in its most simplistic form provides technical
solutions to problems of human use and interactivity. It is also, as I have
been using these terms here, merely data management. It is true, however, that the meaning and value of information *are* a function of information
technology, but in a more complicated way than is often captured by the
commercial business press.

Therefore, the understanding of "information" that I hold throughout
the remainder of the book is much like Agre's notion of a literature: an
always already shaped and networked content, with indeterminate boundaries, of ambivalent power and usefulness. Data I understand to be clearly
discrete and bounded, and chapters 4 and 5 show many interactions with
data. Conversely, "knowledge" I understand to be deeply rhetorical, coordinated in its production and communal in its meaning and value.
However, none of these concepts have much meaning and value once dis-
connected from their infrastructural contexts. This more complicated way
of getting at information though understanding information systems deals
with infrastructure (Star & Ruhleder, 1996; see also the related notions of
classification and standardization in Bowker & Star, 1999). Information
infrastructures shape how we experience information systems and thus
shape what is considered information: what is available, what is possible,
and what we can do. As Bowker and Star (1999) argue, attempts to understand concepts like "information" that are separated from their material
bases and work contexts are difficult if not impossible. For them, "[i]nfor-
mation cannot analytically be released from these contexts" (p. 110).
Therefore, any concern with the design and use of databases and other
information tools for community and civic purposes must begin with mapping, understanding, and including in any design strategy the information
infrastructures in question (my focus in chapter 5). Failure to do so is like
closing the barn door after the horses have escaped, and so one of my pre-
occupations in this book concerns how infrastructures themselves can be
designed.

In defining infrastructure, Star and Ruhleder (1996) ask not *what* an
infrastructure is but *when* it is. Working from a paper by Yrjö Engeström
(1990) that asks "when is a tool," they assert that "infrastructure is something that emerges for people in practice, connected to activities and structures." (p. 112). In other words, just as a tool is not an artifact with "pre-given
attributes frozen in time," but rather is given meaning as a tool by specific

users working on particular problems in specific situations, so too does the meaning and value of an infrastructure emerge. An infrastructure's meaning and use isn't stable. It is a product of ongoing processes of use.

Star and Ruhleder develop the following characteristics of infrastructure:

- *Embeddedness*. Infrastructure is sunk into, inside of, other structures, social arrangements, and technologies.
- *Transparency*. Infrastructure is transparent to use in the sense that it does not have to be reinvented each time or assembled for each task, but invisibly supports those tasks.
- *Reach or scope*. This may be either spatial or temporal—infrastructure has reach beyond a single event or one-site practice.
- *Learned as part of membership*. The taken-for-grantedness of artifacts and organizational arrangements is a sine qua non of membership in a community of practice (Lave & Wenger, 1991, Star, 1996). Strangers and outsiders encounter infrastructure as a target object to be learned about. New participants acquire a naturalized familiarity with its objects as they become members.
- *Links with conventions of practice*. Infrastructure both shapes and is shaped by the conventions of a community of practice; for example, the ways that cycles of day-night work are affected by and affect electrical power rates and needs. Generations of typists have learned the QWERTY keyboard; its limitations are inherited by the computer keyboard and thence by the design of today's computer furniture (Becker, 1982).
- *Embodiment of standards*. Modified by scope and often by conflicting conventions, infrastructure takes on transparency by plugging into other infrastructures and tools in a standardized fashion.
- *Built on an installed base*. Infrastructure does not grow de novo; it wrestles with the inertia of the installed base and inherits strengths and limitations from that base. Optical fibers run along old railroad lines, new systems are designed for backward compatibility; and failing to account for these constraints may be fatal or distorting to new development processes (Montero, Handseth, & Halting, 1994).
- *Becomes visible upon breakdown*. The normally invisible quality of working infrastructure becomes visible when it breaks: the server is down, the bridge washes out, there is a power black-

out. Even when there are backup mechanisms or procedures, their existence further highlights the now visible infrastructure.
- *Is fixed in modular increments, not all at once or globally.* Because infrastructure is big, layered, and complex, and because it means different things locally, it is never changed from above. Changes take time and negotiation, and adjustments with other aspects of the systems involved. (p. 113)

To be more precise, that which is determined to be infrastructural (at a particular time and place) will demonstrate these characteristics. Stated somewhat differently, some configuration of these elements at a particular time and place and for particular users and activities forms a given infrastructure (thus, things like plumbing or rail systems can be very different infrastructures depending on these variables).[4] "Computers, people, and tasks together make or break a functioning infrastructure," Star and Ruhleder write later, further underlining the contingent meanings that can be attached to a concept that is material, institutional, cultural, and social at the same time.

The contingent and dynamic nature of Star and Ruhleder's definition of infrastructure is important. They argue that seeing infrastructure, such as power grids or the Internet, as a static and often transparent background is dangerous. This is true regardless if one's gaze is macro (international network maps) or local (Internet access sites in one community) because "such talk may obscure the ambiguous nature of tools and technologies for different groups, leading to de facto standardization of a single, powerful group's agenda" (p. 114). Infrastructure occurs, Star and Ruhleder write, "when the tension between local and global is resolved," when the dynamic becomes fixed—even for a short period of time—in the form of standards.[5] Thus, although infrastructure is an important, though often invisible, component of institutional or community change, not paying attention to it means to lose the possibilities of influencing that change—or of even understanding it to begin with. As Bowker and Star (1998) assert with respect to the design of computer systems, "[c]ommunity support systems designers make a series of relatively irreversible decisions when they are forced to decide between conflicting representational structures (espoused by conflicting social worlds). These decisions need to be made in full recognition of this fact—and so to be made both as open and as reversible as possible" (p. 239). In other words, infrastructures are designed and given meaning and value within specific contexts (communities, people, tasks). Contingent and designed, infrastructures nonetheless enact, sometimes rigorously, a set of standards—they marry the global and the local—making their design a critical site of intellectual and political activity. Infrastructure, particularly as it relates to "information" and how it shapes what is possible for writers and writing, will be more easy to see by mapping elements of the information infrastructure available to citizens in the United States.

THE FEDERAL DATA SYSTEM

Any inquiry into what information is and how it can be useful to "nonexperts" must first step back and try to grasp what we might call a macro view of the information infrastructure in the United States. Grasping this infrastructure with any precision is probably impossible and would likely require its own book. It would require a mapping of universities, think tanks, nongovernmental organizations, and private corporations and organizations. And it could not reasonably be limited to the United States. Most importantly, it would require mapping local, state, and Federal government efforts. All this would merely suggest who produces the information and tools that form the core of this infrastructure.

It is possible to have a partial understanding of this infrastructure, and to do so I focus on the Federal data system. The Federal data system is something that doesn't attract a great deal of attention, except in those rare instances, such as the sampling controversy that arose during the last census, when data collection catches the attention of mainstream news organizations. But as Crabtree, Chopyak, and Cobb (1999) argue in their paper outlining threats to the Federal data system, such a system is "an essential ingredient in providing a common stock of knowledge that helps to bind a democratic society together" (p. 1). They argue that the public trusts government data more than private data; policy development demands robust data collection and analysis; and no other organization produces and disseminates data of the type and scope produced by the Federal government. Thus, they argue, the Federal data system is critical to civic society:

> It might seem to the casual observer as if statistics just exist on their own. When a newspaper article refers to the number of people who drive to work each day or death rates from cancer, it seldom gives the reader any sense of how such numbers are derived. In fact, a large federal apparatus is required to uncover those basic facts. A few billion

dollars is spent each year to supply the statistics that reveal conditions and trends.

If we want to know the unemployment situation in each city and county or how fast the cost of living is rising, there have to be data collectors paid by the federal government to ask people questions about jobs and prices. If we want to keep food on the table into the next century, we not only need farmers plowing fields; we also need information systems about soil erosion, the financial condition of farmers, and the likely effects of climate change on the grain belt. If we want companies to offer life insurance, the government will need to keep collecting the demographic and other information necessary to predict changes in life expectancy. The availability of data on hundreds of topics is an essential, though almost invisible, part of our society.

Like filling in potholes on city streets, the work of statisticians is a continuous maintenance task of great importance. Statistical work permits problems to be identified and good management decisions to be made. Statistics enable governments to make budgets years in advance, preserve environmental resources, protect the public health, reduce crime, and make intelligent choices about investments in public enterprises. Without the sort of knowledge that statistical agencies provide, achieving collective goals would be difficult or impossible. (pp. 3-4)

Arguments about the power of information to transform people's lives rest primarily on the foundation of data systems, yet they are poorly understood.

For example, there are four statistical agencies that process economic data, and these are the agencies that most would point to as sources of important data about the United States: the Census Bureau and the Bureau of Economic Analysis in the Commerce Department, the Bureau of Labor Statistics in the Labor Department, and the Internal Revenue Service in the Treasury Department. In addition to these four agencies, there are also a number of more focused statistical agencies across the government. Each provides a unique function, not only in terms of the data they produce but the way in which this data is used to drive policy at the Federal level and how this data filters down to local levels. Because it is public data, these databases are among those most easily incorporated into databases intended for public use (and the public uses them—see chapters 4 and 5).

Since 1861, the Government Printing Office (GPO) has been the responsible for federal printing, either directly or through subcontract (US General Accounting Office, 2001). In addition to printing, the GPO is also responsible for the "acquisition, classification, dissemination, and bibliographic control of tangible and electronic government information products" (p. 4). This effectively means that all government agencies must make their publications available to the GPO for cataloging and distribution purposes. This system makes the GPO a key node in the federal data system.

The Federal data system, like many functions of government, is under considerable stress. Crabtree, Chopyak, and Cobb frame the threats to the Federal data system in terms of frugality, deregulation and privatization, devolution, and privacy. Since September 11, 2001, we have to add the impact of increased government secrecy to this list. The threat of frugality seems a chronic condition. Because the data system is funded through discretionary money, it is often subject to drastic cuts in tough budgetary climates (or in ideologically driven efforts to shrink the size of government). Privacy is a threat to the data system because of people's increasing unwillingness to participate in research. Devolution means the transfer of data responsibility to the states, which threatens funding and standardization and therefore threatens the integrity of the data itself. For my purposes, however, the most important threats are from privatization (and related issues of deregulation) and secrecy.

Privatization impacts the data system in at least two ways: the privatization of data collection itself, and the privatization of production and publication (databases, websites). These two issues, of course, overlap considerably. One reason for increased privatization is intellectual property. As I suggested earlier in this chapter, perspectives on the economic value of "information" have shifted significantly, making the massive amounts of information produced through the federal data system more clearly valuable in economic terms. Because of this, and because of initiatives to make the federal government more efficient, functions of the federal data system have been increasingly outsourced. As the Government Accounting Office notes with reference to the production and dissemination functions of the GPO, some of these moves to subcontract functionality are driven by efficiency. But some are driven by changes in information technologies. For example, for some time many federal agencies have been distributing information via their own websites, and since the development of Firstgov, this method has become more common and easier. In such a situation, what is the function of the GPO? While the reasons are different and complex, privatization of the federal data system has been happening for some time; but regardless of the reasons, privatization is also a threat to access, for decision making about privatization affects what the public sees as users. These decision-making processes are critical points in the design of the infrastructure of public information.

As a matter of law, Crabtree, Chopyak, and Cobb (1999) write, the public right to know is official policy (there are three legal mechanisms for this: the Freedom of Information Act, the Copyright Act of 1976, and OMB Circular A-130). They quote from OMB Circular A-130 (revised February 8, 1996) to show the intent of the rule:

> The free flow of information between the government and the public is essential to a democratic society. . . . Because the public disclosure of government information is essential to the operation of a democracy, the management of Federal information resources should protect the public's right of access to government information. . . . Agencies shall: (a) Avoid establishing, or permitting others to establish on their behalf, exclusive, restricted, or other distribution arrangements that interfere with the availability of information dissemination products on a timely and equitable basis; . . . (c) Set user charges for information dissemination products at a level sufficient to recover the cost of dissemination but no higher. They shall exclude from calculation of the charges costs associated with original collection and processing of the information. (Section 7, paragraphs c and f and Section 8, subsection a). (p. 17)

Thus, the government is required to make data available to the public at a reasonable price, usually at the cost of reproduction. In practice, they note, the language and spirit of these legal mechanisms are routinely violated. Some agencies act as if they own copyright for the information and therefore charge license fees and royalties and attempt to restrict redistribution. Redistribution rights are essential for publication on public networks.

Crabtree, Chopyak, and Cobb (1999) were obviously writing before September 11, 2001. There has probably been no greater threat to the public's right to know and the Federal data system than the government's response since September 11 (the organization most effectively tracking this issue is OMB Watch: http://www.ombwatch.org). As one can discover by working through OMB Watch's archives and links, Federal and state government agencies almost immediately began pulling down information that could be considered useful to "terrorists" planning attacks in the United States. This included data on pollution. And since then, government agencies have used the specter of terrorism to justify continued secrecy and denial of freedom of information requests. Threats to public access existed before September 11. In fact, it is worth speculating that some of the current rollback of public information is a function of the political cover provided by the "war on terror."

Access is perhaps most deeply affected by distribution, and distribution is impacted, in turn, by issues of intellectual property. Although the public right to know can be thought of as widespread government policy, and although policy also forbids charging costs beyond dissemination, and although the U.S. government cannot copyright its work, government agencies act differently (Crabtree, Chopyak, & Cobb, 1999). Crabtree, Chopyak, and Cobb (1999) note work (e.g., Gellman, 1995) that has described how agencies have acted as if they have copyright, charged excessive fees, denied access to copies of data, and forced license agreements on users. These problems are only exacerbated when the government privatizes or outsources either data collection and analysis or production. Private organizations are more likely to quickly exert de facto intellectual property rights, if not attempt explicit, legal protections.[6] And these problems become deeper—but unavoidable—with the move to electronic databases and computer networks, either in addition to GPO paper publication for Federal Depository Libraries or instead of them.

How public data is distributed, particularly the design and use of electronic databases, is one focus of my project and another key facet of an information infrastructure. For Crabtree, Chopyak, and Cobb, publication by the GPO (instead of outsourced production, which is less expensive for the government but more expensive for users) and distribution to Federal Depository Libraries is an ideal public access model.[7] They write that Federal agencies were once required to publish through the GPO, which in turn made its publications available to the depository libraries. The authors call this system one of "truly open access" and note that there are 8.6 million visits per year (167,000 people per week) to depository libraries (p. 21). For reasons of technological change, user demands, and, indeed, deregulation and privatization, electronic databases, either on CDs or computer networks, are increasingly common and sometimes replace paper publication in Depository Libraries. Crabtree, Chopyak, and Cobb's solution for access problems is to preserve the paper system, at least as a parallel option. They note that paper access is not only less costly, but that where educational levels are low, paper access is (somehow) easier.[8] Such a solution seems to avoid a critical problem—how to make electronic forms of information easier to access and use.

Indeed, to argue against electronic production and distribution of federal information seems an unproductive strategy. There are significant forces pushing production and distribution in this direction, some of them quite reasonable. The GAO itself, for example, cites a number of challenges to effective electronic production and distribution, many of them concerned with access. The challenge, then, seems to be one of design. As

Bowker and Star (1998) assert, decisions are built into systems like the Federal data system and its networks of production and dissemination. These decisions are often then forgotten and become invisible. They are also often difficult, if not impossible, to reverse. Bowker and Star argue, therefore, that decisions about systems design be made as openly and reversibly as possible. Therefore, attempts to intervene at the point of use are naïve and perhaps useless without a consideration of information infrastructures and institutional systems. Of course, attempts to redesign the federal data system require a design politics on a massive scale. My focus is on local instances of this infrastructure to show where our information comes from, how vital it is to knowledge work in communities, and how fragile the infrastructure really is.

COMMUNITY INFORMATION INFRASTRUCTURES

At various points, local infrastructures link to more macrolevel systems like the federal data system, but they are also quite diverse and, well, local. Their situatedness makes a significant difference in terms of how they figure into the inventional practices of their users, and it is more clear at local levels how design matters. Community computing is ubiquitous. To be sure, some versions of community computing have been fundamental to our understanding and use of the Internet and, therefore, have been with us for a long time (e.g., communities of ideas, identity, and affinity). Here I explore a different, more geographically situated notion of community networking. These types of communities are just as common yet more invisible. Examples of this second type of community network include Prairienet (http://www.prairienet.org/), Camfield Estates in Boston (http://www.camfieldestates.net/), and Northwest Tower in Chicago (http://lcsweb118.lcs.mit.edu/). Each of these projects has a significant connection to a university, but there are also many other types—such as the neighborhoods linked together in Kansas City (http:// www.kcneighbornet.org/)—that exist independent of academic sponsorship. Each is an example of a community network that is linked to localized social networks. Significantly, each network is linked to some notion of community development, social change, or civic engagement. Each project is an attempt to weave the promise of information technologies into the fabric of people's everyday lives.

Community information infrastructures have a history, of course (more than one, actually), as my discussion in chapter 1 shows. These local nodes in this much larger information infrastructure are also amazingly diverse. Thus, Slack (2000) notes that "each implementation of ICTs in the community is unique," which is an appropriate frame for understanding the project in the southeast of Scotland reported by Slack, a project that changed dramatically in both its degree of localization and purpose from its original design (p. 494). van den Besselaar and Beckers (1998) describe in great detail the important Amsterdam Digital City project. They asked if the project resulted in the "emergence of sustainable (local and topical) communities" and if the functions of the Digital City became integrated into people's everyday lives. Their surveys show that the frequency of mutual contact increased between 1994 and 1996, and that over time, information searching became nearly as important a use as email, and much more important than "debate" or virtual interactions. They conclude that mere technological possibility does not determine benefits and outcomes. Design and other contextual issues are more important (p. 109). Similarly de Cindio (2000) recounts the success of community networks in Milan, Italy, concluding as well that context, culture, and design matter a great deal, but that in Milan at least, citizens do, in fact, invent new discourse and media through these networks and that political debate is a widespread activity. Indeed, as Borgida et al. (2002) argue, it is the "civic culture" of a community that impacts how ICT projects will be conceived and succeed. de Cindio sees the Milan network as substantially contributing to the goal of reinventing citizenship in that city. What can get lost in the richness and diversity of these projects is the infrastructural dimension of these initiatives, and, therefore, it is easy to lose sight of both limits and possibilities.

To probe infrastructural dimensions, I turn to Krouk, Pitkin, and Richman (2000), who examine three "emergent" cases illustrating Internet-based systems that support community planning. Their criteria for selecting their emergent cases lay bare the power of local information infrastructures. The criteria they use for selection of their cases mark an initiative as a "neighborhood information system" if it

1. Incorporates an Internet-based system that provides public access to property and demographic related information.
2. Provides access to record and/or statistical data at the neighborhood level.
3. Provides an interpretive framework for its information, aimed at nonprofessionals. (p. 278)

Based on these criteria, they selected the Center for Neighborhood Technology's Neighborhood Early Warning System (NEWS) in Chicago, Neighborhood Knowledge Los Angeles (NKLA) in Los Angeles, and the Public Access Network in Seattle. Each of these projects is complex and substantial in its own right, far beyond even the treatment that Krouk, Pitkin, and Richman provide. Here I want to focus on these initiatives as nodes in an infrastructure. The NEWS project in Chicago relies on access to the City of Chicago's mainframe and the databases found there. NKLA is similarly connected to the City of Los Angeles and makes a point of accessing "difficult to access databases," such as building code complaints and property tax records. The Seattle project is a massive planning-related data initiative and so provides residents with access to a full set of planning data sets. Such access is critical to the success of these projects, but two significant problems are common to each: difficulty in obtaining and updating databases, and effective use by their audience, particularly those considered "grassroots" users. Thus, threats to the federal data system are also threats to community data systems; citizen access to their own information is embedded in a tremendously complex infrastructure that both enables and limits how they can be productive—how and what they can write— with the support of this infrastructure. This infrastructure is global and local, technological and cultural, and an expression and determinant of various civic cultures. In one sense, then, this discussion of infrastructure establishes the scene for rhetorical activity, but even this is too passive. This information infrastructure is both scene and participant, both the tool and the object of our attention and rhetorical intervention.

BORING THINGS

One purpose of this chapter has been to map, however partially, certain nodes and strands of the information infrastructure that supports the work of citizens in the United States. Another purpose has been to establish information infrastructures as part of the scene of civic rhetoric. Not only must people use information infrastructures to act as citizens, but the infrastructure itself must become the object of our design attention. That is, if certain technologies, interfaces, or moments in an information infrastructure are difficult to use, if access is limited and limiting, then the infrastructure itself must become the object of our attention.

Another purpose of this chapter is to establish how this notion of infrastructure enables deeper understandings of information. Here again my interest is in how an information infrastructure supports the work of citizenship. For me, the concept of infrastructure *locates* information, and the value of locating (as distinct from defining) is that it makes it difficult to make wildly utopic claims about the power, meaning, and value of information itself. It prevents the separation of information from material and social bases. It demands that information be given its history (back) and its utility located in various communities of practice. Thus, if we look again at how I have tried to map elements of the data system as part of an information infrastructure, it is possible to see both the existence and interrelatedness of elements we might otherwise miss or see as discrete. We can see that databases and the systems of data collection and analysis that lead to databases are deeply embedded in the practices of government and an array of organizations—some of them citizen organizations—that rely on federal data. As I show in later chapters, the importance of good information to make persuasive arguments in communities is essential. A constant question is what makes information credible. In ways both material and rhetorical, the federal data system is both embedded in the practices of citizen organizations and largely transparent in its support of these organizations. It is also true that the standards that support the information infrastructures in communities have considerable reach and are a function of conventions. This is possible to see in the debates about data collection standards and the appropriate design and dissemination of databases. The problem with an information infrastructure like the federal data system and its links with community information systems is that these standards and classifications are determined by experts. Thus, as again I show in later chapters, we run into significant problems when specialist technologies and information migrate to nonspecialist users. That is, tools that support the writing of experts can quickly become impediments to the writing of nonexperts (which all of us are, again, when we find ourselves writing in strange contexts with information we struggle to understand to audiences we do not know). As Agre's (1995) work on information also shows, information per se does not exist, ready formed and understandable to users. "Information" is embedded in an infrastructure, and like scholars learning to map, access, and understand a literature, the ability to find and use information for community writing is a significantly difficult and rhetorical act. And as Johnson-Eilola (2005) writes about relationships between "information" and the acts of the "writers" he is referencing,

> Rather than understanding creativity as the inspired production of solitary genius, these users manipulated pre-existing data, filtering, cutting, pasting, moving. Rather than seeing information as something they needed to master and contain, they saw information as a rich field in which to work. I was struck, that is, by the possibilities of computer use as something that broke open and radically transformed traditional ways of working and living. (p. 3)

And so the violence of the myth that information somehow exists and is useful to people is that it masks the activity of making use of an information infrastructure. We in fact create information out of our interactions with infrastructures. In computers and writing and related fields we would understand this activity as "writing" and the concepts guiding this activity as "rhetoric."

If we focus on the concept of infrastructure rather than the concept of information, then our attention shifts radically to what is indeed useful for individuals and communities as they seek to generate persuasive discourse about what is good, true, and possible. It becomes impossible to decontextualize information and see it as useful. It also becomes apparent that simplistic notions of access are an inadequate public policy response to the need for useful information communication technologies. Perhaps most importantly, it shifts our design gaze to deep issues and problems. Infrastructures are not just the information, not just the interfaces, not just the computers or the wires. Infrastructures enact standards, they are activity systems, and they are also people themselves (and all that people entail, such as cultural and communal practices, identities, and diverse purposes and needs). Community networks of any kind are social, political, and technical; they get work done and allow others to work; and they embody a set of often hidden and invisible design decisions and standards that change people and communities. It's not information that is powerful. Infrastructures are powerful. As Star (1999) writes

> The ecological effect of studying boring things (infrastructure, in this case) is in some ways similar. The ecology of the distributed high-tech workplace, home, or school is profoundly impacted by the relatively unstudied infrastructure that permeates all its functions. Study a city and neglect its sewers and power supplies (as many have), and you miss essential aspects of distributional justice and planning power (Latour & Hermant, 1998). Study an information system and neglect its standards, wires, and settings, and you miss equally essential aspects of aesthetics, justice, and change. Perhaps if we stopped thinking of computers as information highways and began to think of them more modestly as symbolic sewers, this realm would open up a bit. (p. 379)

As I demonstrate in the chapters that follow, this project is very much a study of boring things. Writing to prevent a dump or trying to access information through a simple website or crafting a letter to a city council person is pretty boring stuff to most people. But these writing practices are how communities change, and those interested in increasing the capacity of others to act effectively must see infrastructures—the boring things that support mundane work—as terribly important and exciting.

NOTES

1. Street's (1984) critique of the literacy and development link implicates the United Nations, and indeed, the UN is perhaps the most important place to look for historical and contemporary discussions of literacy in the context of human development. More recent UN indicators utilizing literacy seem more subtle. See an example set of indicators here (latest access 8/15/05): http://www.un.org/esa/sustdev/natlinfo/indicators/isd.htm

2. See as well a current United Nations indicator for "information access" (latest access 8/15/05) http://www.un.org/esa/sustdev/natlinfo/indicators/isdms2001 /isd-ms2001institutional.htm#inhabitants1000

3. The knowledge management literature is perhaps a perfect example for my purposes here. Part of that literature is a serious attempt to understand macrolevel economic changes and their microlevel organizational implications given the shift in the developed world from manufacturing to service/information industries. Part of the literature is trendy, thin, and relatively uninteresting if not wrong (see Brown & Duguid, 2000, for this critique). All knowledge management work ignores the complexities of communication.

4. Star and Ruhleder (1996) explain this difference by pointing out that a plumbing system is the object of attention for a plumber, but just one element of a larger system for a civil engineer or city planner.

5. According to Bowker and Star (1988), classifications and standards do work (i.e., they allow people to do work), and they define them in this way: "Classifications and standards are two sides of the same coin. The distinction between them (as we are defining them) is that classifications are containers for the descriptions of events—they are an aspect of organizational, social, and personal memory—whereas standards are procedures for how to do things—they are an aspect of acting in the world. Every successful standard imposes a classification system" (p. 234).

6. There are situations in which value is added to public data, therefore, a case can be made for private property rights—the case of legal research seems a prime example. See Crabtree, Chopyak, and Cobb (1999, pp. 21-28) for more on forms of privatization and their impacts on intellectual property.

7. OMB Circular A-130 was revised by the Reagan administration to ensure that the government did not duplicate information systems available in the private sector, and every effort was to be used to allow the private sector to disseminate information. This same circular was revised under the Bush (I) and then the Clinton administrations to focus on government dissemination at cost. Further revision of this circular bears watching for its implications for public access to information.

8. Paper or "tangible" production and distribution is still required when any one of the following conditions is met: (1) it is legally required; (2) it is of significant reference value to depository libraries; (3) it serves a special needs population; (4) it is the commonly accepted medium of the user community; (5) it is essential to the conduct of government (US Government Accounting Office, 2001, p. 7).

3

COMMUNITY INFORMATION AND RISK COMMUNICATION

METHODOLOGY OF TWO CASES

Two studies constitute the empirical substance of this book. The studies are different in many respects. They are located in two different communities and have distinct origins and purposes. Yet they are linked in that they demonstrate how people write with advanced information technologies to support their work in communities. This chapter details the methodologies of these two studies, and, in so doing, provides background that will be useful for understanding the discussion in subsequent chapters.

As I wrote in the first chapter, this book is an attempt to represent new methodological directions. The two studies I discuss have been in process for some time now and are intended to pay attention to how people are working communities over time. The first study is a risk communication project examining, in part, how citizens "did science" and communicated that science. The second study is about the design and use of a community information resource.

The methodological link for these two studies is my understanding of "action research" (AR) and how it might be enacted in rhetoric and writing. The fact that AR is possible across the fields invoked in this book is something that I do not take for granted. It is a significant methodological strength of these fields. In computers and writing, there exists significant work on power and access (e.g., Grabill, 1998; Janangelo, 1991; Moran, 1999; Regan, 1993; Selfe, 1999; Selfe & Selfe, 1994), including some work on critical research (Takayoshi, 2000), the writing practices of people in communities (Regan & Zuern, 2000), and workers who are not commonly considered "knowledge workers" (Rohan, 2003).

There is a similar critical research tradition in technical and professional writing, another field in which I situate my work. The most comprehensive reviews of critical research in technical and professional writing are provided by Blyler (1998) and Herndl and Nahrwold (2000). Their critique is that much of the research conducted in technical and professional writing merely describes the workplace writing scene. Too little engages in critique and intervention. They argue that descriptive research supports, either implicitly or explicitly, the interests of those who sponsor research. Critics of descriptive research argue that it often leaves in place and unquestioned ideological and cultural practices and therefore prevents more complex understandings of discursive practices and the institutions that warrant them. The usefulness of the critical research traditions in both computers and writing and technical and professional writing is the possibility for shared work and problem solving as the basis for an inquiry and the theoretical support to play out, through research practices, the implications of long-standing methodological issues: the neutrality and objectivity of the researcher; the goals and purposes of research; and the rhetorical nature of research itself.

As I have written previously (Grabill, 2003a), I also look to community-based research for methodological guidance for conducting AR projects. Community-based research, at least in the ways that community-based researchers talk about it, does not differ much, if at all, from ways that writing researchers think about their own work. There is a concern with power and ethics, with why research is conducted, by whom, in whose interests, and to what ends. There is a concern with representation and identity in both the research and writing processes. There is also vigilance and self-reflection in terms of understanding what motivates and sponsors research. Community-based research is generally thought of as research that involves citizens working with professionally trained researchers in a community-driven process to answer local questions or solve local problems. Much like discussions of the role of participants in writing research, community-based researchers focus on developing the relationships necessary to engage community members in the practices of research, analysis, and writing. Community-based research is also action driven, and so community outreach activities like education, political and social change, and policymaking are often explicit project goals. Community-based research is not without its conceptual and practical problems, as reflected in common questions such as these: Is research done on community members or with them? Are community members supplying questions and initiating research projects or not? Are community members primary participants or merely consultants? Conducting community-based research is extremely difficult because communities must be well organized, researchers must be open and flexible to working in new ways, and meaningful participation is difficult to achieve.

I have always understood action research in light of the interests of fields like computers and writing, technical and professional writing, and community-based research. In addition, I understand action research as connected to approaches called "participatory action research." Action research and participatory action research are articulated differently due to the fact that practitioners work in diverse ideological and material conditions (e.g., Bangladesh or Denmark or Brazil). Researchers invoking the action research tradition work in corporations to improve efficiency and workflow, in the developing world on agricultural policies and practices, and in projects redesigning cities in the developed world. I have found this diversity both humbling and invigorating, but despite the apparent differences, action researchers tend to hold to some simple and powerful commitments. Action researchers think of themselves as working with people to answer questions and solve problems—as opposed to researching "on" people and their problems. The resulting research projects tend to move among theorizing, capacity building, and problem solving, and, again, can be remarkably diverse. As Schafft and Greenwood (2003) write,

> projects may include capacity building, theory and hypothesis development, conventional research activities, action design and ongoing evaluation of outcomes in which the local knowledge of the relevant stakeholders makes as much a contribution to the process as the professional knowledge of the outside social researchers makes. (p. 23)

As enacted in the two projects I discuss here, my approach to action research has been shaped by the conceptual work I have represented here, but also by the particular situations in which the projects exist and my own specific interests. Both projects are examples of complex collaborative and coordinated work. The risk communication project in Harbor is sponsored by an outreach group in civil and environmental engineering at Michigan State University, and as a researcher engaged by this group, my work is coordinated with and by them and shaped by other project constraints as well. In addition, the inquiry has been collaboratively conducted with my colleague Stuart Blythe. The Capital Area Community Information project has less clear institutional sponsorship. The project has come together because of some generous help from key individuals not directly participating in the project, the willing and generous collaboration of other individuals involved in the project, and some funding by Michigan State

University's office of Outreach and Engagement and The Writing in Digital Environments (WIDE) research center at Michigan State University. All these variables impact quite dramatically what an action research project looks like and what it can accomplish. And as I wrote in chapter 1, I am very much interested in action research that achieves its pragmatic goals and is capable of meaningful theoretical work as well. In this regard, I have drawn a set of research practices from community-based researchers and applied anthropologists, two communities of researchers who wrestle with issues of location, audience, and the impact of their research on the two. These practices constitute a set of categories that are not new to research methodology. At the same time, however, they are sometimes invisible given the ways we talk about research methodology:

1. Initiation: or where do studies come from?
2. Access: or how do I get permission to do my work?
3. Participation (with sponsors, clients, all those impacted; in planning, design, method, analysis, and communication)
4. Studying up (or studying one's client or sponsor as well)
5. Local politics (mediation, advocacy, relationship building and maintenance, community and political mapping)
6. Communication (as a day-to-day research practice itself, as well as in myriad settings during the research process regarding "nonresearch issues"—all in addition to the communication of the research results themselves)
7. Sustainability

Elsewhere, I explore the meaning of some of these research practices (Grabill, 2006). Here I want to highlight the importance of four of these—studying up, local politics, communication, and sustainability—for my own methodological practice. In my discussion of each project, I try to point out where these practices are involved. Here I highlight them because they are central to the "action" part of the research process. That is, in each project, there are moments when we are trying to enable "studying up," sometimes by helping community partners understand us and how we work institutionally. Sometimes we do this by collectively focusing our gaze on more powerful institutional players. At almost every moment in these projects, we are involved in local political practices. Indeed, I have long understood the work I do in communities *as* politics, mostly in an Aristotelian sense of imagining and enacting what is possible. But sometimes in more practical ways as well, as in knowing that our work on a given project will help a partner with political work she is doing elsewhere in the community. The fact that we research communication means that we should be attentive to the ways in which research itself communicates and the ways in which action-based projects must generate communication results in the middle of a project. And finally, one of the reasons for trying to "pay attention" over time is to build meaningful sustainability into projects so that work continues under new collaborative and coordinated relationships.

Having written a few words about how research should proceed or be conducted, it is important to note that research almost never proceeds in these ways. Particularly with action-based approaches that depend on participation, the tendency in the literature is to idealize the research scene. I attempt here and elsewhere in the book to resist this tendency. As I discuss later in this chapter, the idea of "the community" is just that—an idea—just as concepts like "participation" are often more ideas than actual activity in methodological discussions (see Schafft & Greenwood, 2003). In my experience, figuring out who or what the community is remains a persistent problem throughout a project and is ultimately the construction of the researcher (or the community organizer). Participation, collaboration, and coordination are always difficult, and widespread participation in a community is rare in my experience. Furthermore, community dynamics around a research project are often similar to the dynamics that already exist in the community. This means that sometimes research practices are impacted by—indeed become a part of—interpersonal and organization politics and prejudices. It has also been my experience that the value of a research project for my collaborators often varies widely. For some the problem solving is most important. For others, the questions we are trying to answer are essential. For still others it is the capacity building, and for many it is some element of the process itself that they find engaging (for a similar take, see Ray & Barton, 1998). All this is one way to say that the complex and sometimes disappointing dynamics of community work are normal, but it is also what makes the research compelling and humbling—but never ideal. I proceed, then, with a methodological description and argument for each study.

RISK COMMUNICATION IN HARBOR

I have been working for just over two years now on a risk communication project in the community of Harbor, a city that has as much industrial density as any area in North America.[1] In Harbor, there exists a short, man-made river channel that links various industrial operations with a lake. Periodically, this channel must be dredged to allow for barge traffic. Given the industrial density in Harbor over a prolonged period of time, the sediments in the channel are heavily polluted. Currently, these sediments flow into the lake, polluting that water body. Thus, for navigational and environmental reasons, the channel must be dredged. Dredging these sediments, however, creates another set of problems, as the dredging operation threatens to resuspend contaminants in the water. Furthermore, the transportation of the sediments creates risks, as does the disposal and treatment of the sediments, currently planned to take place in an open confined disposal facility (or CDF—essentially a landfill protected by clay walls). The project is planned for thirty years, so it is a project of some size. The confined disposal facility will remain open—that is, uncapped—for those thirty years, meaning that there is also a risk of air pollution due to blowing dust particles. To make matters more difficult, the confined disposal facility is located within a few hundred yards of two schools.

Currently there are two federal agencies, one state agency, two local governments (with their various management and technical functions), four universities, and a number of community-based organizations (some fluid, some stable) involved in deliberations regarding the project. The project touches on issues of engineering (civil, chemical, and environmental), dredging technologies and operations, public health assessment, airborne contaminant research, geology, and a host of legal, procedural, and ethical issues. The citizen groups participating in the decision-making processes associated with this project are at a considerable disadvantage, particularly given the fact that they do not have the resources to hire their own experts.

I am working as part of a team of university-based experts and with a larger group of people in Harbor. Stuart Blythe and I are "communication experts" working for Technical Outreach Services to Communities (TOSC). TOSC is the outreach arm of our EPA region's Hazardous Substances Research Center (HSRC). Our Center is located at Purdue University with capacity located at Michigan State University and Kansas State University. This arrangement is not uncommon for an HSRC, and every HSRC has a TOSC unit. TOSC's mission is to facilitate public involvement by providing independent technical expertise to communities. EPA asked TOSC to work in Harbor because of the high level of distrust between community groups and the U.S. Army Corps of Engineers—and EPA itself. This arrangement is significant to the project. Citizens in Harbor have little use for the Army Corps of Engineers and distrust EPA as well. Because TOSC is funded by EPA (the HSRC grant) and because EPA requested that TOSC help residents in Harbor, TOSC itself was not trusted initially and still is not fully trusted by many in the community. This is not a project that has unfolded as an ideal action research project (it is probably typical, however). TOSC was not exactly invited by the community, and TOSC's mission requires it to remain politically "neutral" as a technical and scientific outreach organization. Stuart and I were asked to work on this project because TOSC realized that they were confronting deep problems that were fundamentally communicative in nature, namely, how does one work effectively in or with communities marked by significant distrust and broken relationships? In fact, having communication researchers as part of a TOSC team is highly unusual. More common are the other specialists on this project: a specialist in contaminated sediments, one in air-borne toxins, and one in CDF design.

Nevertheless, Stuart and I have been conducting what we think of as an action research project that is framed by some simple questions and goals, which reflect the two action components of our project: to help TOSC work in the community and help community organizations solve problems.[2] Our goals are to

1. Create relations of trust with community organizations to enable TOSC to do its work.
2. Create relations of trust with community organizations to facilitate the communicative work of these organizations.
3. Help TOSC create good communication strategies and tools; strategies that are both ethical and effective.

Our questions are similarly simple and reinforce the action goals:

1. Who is the community (around this project)?
2. How do you understand the project?
3. How do you do your research?
4. How do you communicate your research?

Our action and research goals are interrelated. The questions reflect genuine unknowns and problems that we need to figure out if we are going to be able to help both TOSC and our community partners work more effectively. As an action-based project, the rhythms of the project have been related to the tempo of TOSC's outreach activities. After an initial phase of interviews and meeting attendance in which Stuart and I focused on mapping the community and listening to how people understood and were concerned by the dredging project, our work tended to cluster around the preparation and dissemination of a TOSC report or a request in the community for our attendance at a meeting, usually just to listen.[3]

Thus, what we would describe as the "tactics" of the project included standard research practices—in our case interviews and observation—as well as the production of TOSC technical reports. As an outreach organization, TOSC is extremely interesting. It produces new science, often in the form of technical and scientific reviews of existing science.[4] Then it communicates these results in ways meant to be accessible and useful to the community. As I describe in chapters 4 and 5, one of the most significant reasons for the lack of trust in Harbor is the way in which communication practices—meetings, reporting, the use of documents—were used for manipulative purposes or were perceived to have been manipulative by people in attendance at community meetings even if the intent was not malignant. Stuart and I worked on new meeting and reporting tactics for TOSC in an effort to help TOSC communicate in a way that was (a) different from past communication practices of the Army and EPA, (b) consistent with TOSC's best practices, yet (c) attentive to the ways in which organizations communicate within the community and prefer to be engaged by outsiders (see chapter 5). With respect to the production of TOSC reports and the conduct of community meetings, we changed how TOSC wrote reports (by our presence in the writing process), how they distributed reports, and how public meetings were conducted in Harbor. This is a community that craved good science and the help of others in their effort to work toward a more healthy community. Their problems were not with science or expertise or outsiders *per se*; their problem was with how outsiders behaved.

We have collected lots of data. We monitor the press, collect relevant government documents, collect relevant scientific and technical reports, and collect, finally, what TOSC produces, both internally and externally. In addition, we have conducted a number of interviews and kept notes from public meetings, organizational meetings, and other, related interactions in the community. Stuart and I have been analyzing this data for some time, coding these various types of data in ways consistent with the four research questions listed earlier.[5] We have consistently fed results back into the project, almost always to argue for changing the ways that TOSC conducts itself. This use of communication as a research practice has been an important part of the action research as it has impacted TOSC.

I report outcomes or results in later chapters, particularly the ways in which organizations in Harbor use advanced information technologies to write. Here I want to present two significant outcomes that impact the coherence of the material to be presented later in the book. The first and perhaps most significant outcome is the fact that TOSC is still active and working in Harbor some two years after the project began. Given the levels of mistrust in Harbor and the specific ways that TOSC was tagged as "government" (and therefore "not a good neighbor to us," as one individual liked to put it), it is indeed significant that TOSC is still functioning in Harbor. I attribute this to the quality of the communication-related work TOSC has done. This is not exclusive to Stuart and me by any means. And it is not exclusive to the products either (the reports). Rather, it is as much a function of the action research process: a commitment to listen, to try to imagine and work on shared problems, to communicate consistently and honestly, and to being present in the community regularly. The most significant problem we knew we had to solve was the problem of trust, and we used the process and practices of research themselves to address this issue. The other outcome necessary to report here is our best effort at a community map. I report it in the methodology discussion because the production of such maps is a necessary part of any community-based research, and a map such as this (see Fig. 3.1) sets up the argument I make in detail throughout the rest of the book: that the work of citizenship is knowledge work conducted by organizations (individuals collaborating or coordinating their work).

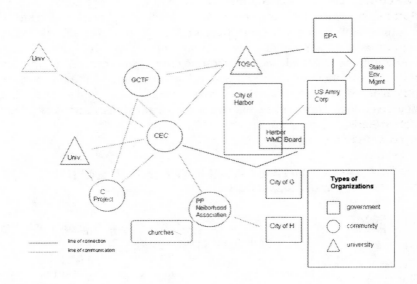

Fig. 3.1. What is a community?

Figure 3.1 is my answer to the question "who/what is the community" in Harbor—at least it is the answer as of April 2004, the date of this figure in fieldnotes. There are two significant issues this map is meant to communicate. The first is that the community, as I see it forming around this particular project at this time, is a collection of organizations, institutions, and individuals (individuals are not visible in this version of the map). This is important because work in communities is sufficiently complex to require coordinated work, and so it should be no surprise that people organize themselves to conduct this work. To be sure, some of these organizations are large and highly structured, like a government agency, whereas others are more loosely structured, such as a neighborhood association. My claim, however, is that "community" is fluid and can be articulated along the vectors of time, place, and project (or work/activity). Furthermore, I am claiming that work in communities is completed by groups of people and that these people are organized in recognizable ways. The second issue I want this map to highlight is links between groups. Some groups have more formal connections, by way of funding or people who are members of multiple organizations, for example. Some groups are networked by their communication practices. The organization named "CEC" is the key community organization in my discussion of Harbor because we have experienced them as located at the very center of communication practices—and therefore coordinated work—in Harbor. Although small and relatively unstructured, they are highly effective communicators: they write frequently and with impact; have multiple, effective communication channels; and use both to share what they learn and, thus, receive from others what they are learning. I intend this map as a useful data display for my purposes in this chapter, but it is also worth remembering in later chapters as context for more fine-grained discussions of writing work in Harbor.

CAPITAL AREA COMMUNITY INFORMATION

The Capital Area Community Information (CACI) project is an example of a "community informatics" project as described in chapter 1 and also an attempt to both understand and make infrastructure. It is a project focused on designing with "users" (citizens) information communication technologies that will support their knowledge work in communities. CACI is a study of an existing digital government effort called CACVoices (http:// www.cacvocies.org), and includes both the public website that hosts databases and other types of public information and the community organizations that contribute to and rely on that resource. This section provides background on the CACI project, beginning with history of the CACVoices initiative.

In 2000, the City of Lansing and the Ingham County Health Department signed agreements to collaborate in creating web resources to inform residents about issues vital to community well being. The goal of this effort was to increase the use of data and information in decision making by residents. It was thought that the best way to do this was to create an open, collaborative system in which users from various community groups could add and modify content themselves. This agreement is the origin of the CACVoices website, which is the focus of the CACI project.

The main component of the community data systems found at CACVoices consists of vital records and statutory databases. These are collected automatically and in designated ways year after year by agencies. Birth certificates and well water tests are good examples. Although the CACVoices resource is run by the Public Health Department, many community organizations continue to provide tangible support, making it the key community data and information resource. Most significantly, the Capital Area United Way, the City of Lansing, the Lansing Police Department, the Mid Michigan GIS Consortium, and several local school districts participate. In addition, twenty-two community-based organizations are working on CACVoices or developing their own web pages on the site. These organizations form the basis of the user community that I discuss later in the study design.

Although the CACVoices resource is valued by community-based organizations in the Capital Area, it has had less impact than both institutional sponsors and community organizations would like. The results from our initial, interview-based inquiry with users shows that available communication tools are not well-known, understood, or utilized.[6] Furthermore, interviews suggest deep and pervasive usability problems with interfaces and database tools. There is no evidence as yet that the information tools have enabled citizen productivity, interaction with government, or that they have led to the social transformation expected by both sponsors and users.

Like many data-rich interfaces, this one provides a confusing array of options and languages for nonexpert users (see Fig. 3.2). Once users find and access specific database tools, they are confronted with interfaces and language that demand expert users (see Fig. 3.3). The problems suggested by these interfaces are substantial, both at the interface (usability) and in terms of their implications for what users can do with the information (usefulness). With respect to "usability," the project maintains an important con-

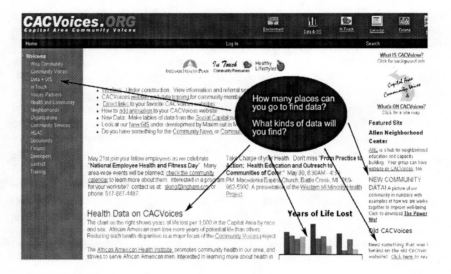

Fig. 3.2. Welcome screen for CACVoices

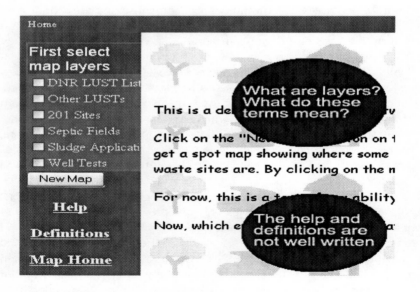

Fig. 3.3. The ground water contamination database interface

ceptual distinction between *usability*, or task-focused and time-limited use that takes place primarily at the computer interface, and *usefulness*, or the uses to which individuals and organizations put information and information technology tools in the interests of their own goals and productive tasks. The key point is that we know that CACVoices, like many other digital government initiatives, has fundamental problems related to its use by nonexpert, citizen audiences. However, at the beginning of the project, we didn't know, exactly, the full extent and depth of the usability problems that confront this project. At this point I'm not sure we yet understand what type of design theory will best facilitate usefulness, meaningful collaboration, and good writing. In this book, I report some initial answers to these questions.

By focusing on both usability and usefulness in successive years of the project, the CACI project focuses on human use by applying usability methods informed by community-based research practices. That is, we hope to use the methods employed to study the coordinated writing of citizen organizations as *the* fundamental measure of a system's usefulness. At the same time, the action component is focused on providing better tools and increasing community capacity.

The study design unfolded over three years. Year one established baseline data on local information technology capacity and use and identified usability problems with CACVoices. Year two featured more substantial usability research, in both lab and community-based settings. In year two, we also worked with individuals and organizations in the community on information development, training, and capacity building with respect to productivity with information technologies. In year three, we have been working with users as they continue to use CACI, add information and resources to it, and write. Throughout the project, we ran a test version of the complete CACI infrastructure on a separate server to prevent research from interfering in the ongoing work of CACVoices and permit ongoing development.[7]

Throughout each iteration of the project, we studied the resources both individuals and groups used to achieve their goals, both within and outside the CACVoices site. We used these data to construct affinity diagrams that aggregate goals, resources, and tasks in order to map these to functions CACVoices could provide or do a better job supporting. But, as we expect to go beyond the methods traditionally associated with contextual inquiry and user-centered design in order to address the unique challenge of citizen-centered design, the project also used community and asset mapping strategies to help develop with individuals and organizations a shared sense of needs and goals (e.g., Kretzmann & McKnight, 1993).

In addition, we have been working with individuals and organizations in the community to assist capacity building with respect to the changing CACI interfaces and tools. In addition, the project is leveraging the resources of the professional writing program and the WIDE Center to assist the productive capacity of individuals and organizations to produce media and documents for CACI (e.g., websites, new media pieces, and other sorts of professional documentation). We understand these engagement activities to be epistemologically rich; they will produce new knowledge central to the project. It is also an important connection to the university curriculum. Ultimately we are interested in the collaborative functionality of CACVoices, in the ability of people to design and use their own tools for supporting the knowledge work of citizenship. Will the design theories developed and implemented during the course of the project lead to greater use, more effective use, and demonstrable social transformation in CACI communities? We hope to answer this question. In this book I offer some tentative answers focused on how people write to effect community change and based on our initial tool and infrastructure-building efforts.

Despite the differences in these projects, I trust that it is possible to see connections between them. More important are the ways that these studies enable descriptions of the complex work required of citizens. Furthermore, I intend this chapter as an argument for a type of sustained action research in communities, projects that enable citizens to understand practices of power and use powerful technologies.

What may be more difficult to see is that I am interested in "writing" and, moreover, writing (with) advanced information technologies. I am trying to show how deeply these technologies and acts of writing have penetrated the day-to-day work of citizenship. Writing (and) technologies *are* infrastructure. And so although I intend to explore these issues much more deeply, I don't intend to make it less difficult to "see" writing in ways that we are accustomed to seeing it. I want us to see writing and working in communities much differently—and less romantically—than is typical. If we want to make a difference, we must do the hard work of studying mundane things and paying attention to them for a long time.

NOTES

1. The name "Harbor" as well as the names of all individuals and organizations associated with the community are pseudonyms.

2. A number of colleagues have pointed out that these goals are contradictory. My response has always been that these goals are *potentially* contradictory. There is an important conversation that has yet to take place in the larger field of rhetoric and writing that is captured by my qualification here. That conversation would be concerned with asking for more nuanced, complex, and "real" discussions of empirical methodologies in communities and in other situations marked by asymmetries of power. It would be concerned with the inescapable role of institutions in shaping the research scene. And this conversation would also tackle the critical problem of how our work can have an impact beyond our necessarily narrow disciplinary conversations. I always understood the opportunity to work in Harbor as less than ideal and fraught with potential problems, and I also knew that many of these potential problems were beyond my direct control. I also knew that we could make a difference in Harbor. When confronted with potentially contradictory situations such as this, what are we supposed to do as researchers? Refuse to participate because of all the embedded problems? Participate and run the risk of doing harm? In such a situation, which is the side of the angels?

3. Our offer to help the organizations with whom we were meeting with their own communication issues—an offer of reciprocity—was consistently ignored, initially, in part, because people didn't trust us. We also learned later how effective one organization, in particular, was at communication. They didn't need our assistance. Over time, our value to some community organizations was our willingness to listen carefully and pass information to our colleagues at TOSC as a way of influencing TOSC's actions. We focused on this research practice as a way of "studying up," or helping individuals understand how TOSC functioned and what we thought was possible.

    In the first chapter, I described studying up in terms of Cintron's dragon and the research practices found in applied anthropology. Conceptually, *studying up* means studying the powerful, not the marginal. In Harbor, we did this by helping one community group understand TOSC, and, to the best of our ability, what we could understand about the EPA. This studying took many forms. I would share with Barbara what I learned on conference calls she did not attend. More often I would share interpretations of key individuals, organizational dynamics, motivations, and so on within TOSC and with respect to TOSC's interactions with other institutions. I would talk on the phone with Barbara, a citizen in Harbor, and sit in her living room puzzling her own organization's strategy. All of these practices are part of the less visible study of us, not of Harbor.

4. I doubt that many of the scientists with whom I have worked on this project would understand a technical review as producing new science. Such an interpretation of existing data sets and on-the-ground conditions is often perceived as outreach or consulting. However, it is quite clear that the reports produced by TOSC impact the scientific debate of a project. Furthermore, TOSC reports are clearly perceived as "science" by those in the Harbor community and valued as such.

5. Our coding scheme had two parts to it. Each "rhetorical unit," which could be a sentence (a claim or argument), paragraph, portion of a document, or entire document, was assigned a code for "speaker" (citizens, experts, Corps, government, or journalist) and a code for purpose: an environmental characterization of the project, a health-focused characterization, an economic characterization, a political characterization, a moral characterization, or a characterization focused on justice; we also coded for descriptions of how data and information is gathered, claims of credibility, and claims of certainty; we also coded for descriptions or moments of community organizing, citizen communication practices, and statements about community identity. This is a complex coding scheme. The most significant problem was the notion of a rhetorical unit, and the most significant disagreements between us concerned the length of a given unit.

6. As in the Harbor project, the "we" involved is quite complex. Project "sponsors" include John Melcher of Michigan State University's Community and Economic Development Program for generously enabling access to community organizations and related institutions. The Ingham County Public Health Department, which supports CACVoices, has been a fundamental sponsor of this work, as have numerous individuals within the Health Department. In addition, the project has been underwritten by a grant from Michigan State University's Office of Outreach and Engagement and by the Writing in Digital Environments Research Center at Michigan State. Active collaborators include LeRoy Harvey, a community member and long-time participant in local data democratization and capacity-building projects; Marcus Cheatham, a Public Health Department statistician and leader of data democratization in the Lansing area; Sarah Swereinga, the Director of Michigan State University's Usability and Accessibility Center; and Amy Diehl, a graduate student in the Digital Rhetoric and Professional Writing Program, who has been a tremendously smart researcher and excellent collaborator.

7. The existence of this project within the Writing in Digital Environments infrastructure has had an interesting consequence. It has piqued the interest of graduate students and fed the development of new tools built on open source architectures and intended for use in communities. We hope to give away these tools in the near future and report on how they are used.

4

INVENTING (IN) A COMMUNITY

My argument in this book is that the work of citizenship is knowledge work, meaning that people in communities must coordinate their work, use specialist technologies to write, and write about issues that are considered scientific, technical, or otherwise demanding some form of expertise. The work of citizenship, I have also argued, is supported by a complex information infrastructure, and to this point I have suggested that this infrastructure is both fragile and poorly designed to support knowledge work in communities.

What I haven't done to this point in the book is show what this knowledge work looks like. I haven't shown how people engage in coordinated, technologically rich acts of writing. I do so in this chapter. My approach is to blend a discussion of how people write with advanced information technologies into an argument for a particular rhetorical way of understanding these writing processes. In this way, I insist that the knowledge work of citizens in communities be understood as epistemologically rich and entailing complex inventional practices.[1] Just as important to my argument about the rhetorical work of citizens is the *type* of knowledge invented in and by communities. As I wrote in the first chapter, it is not enough to say that people should participate in public deliberations or that they are capable of knowing things. In order to persuasively argue for change, the knowledge produced in communities must be shown to be expert in some way, to be capable of contesting the rhetorics of expert institutions. Thus, in this and the next chapter I am also concerned with the value of the work done by citizens, which means dealing with issues of expertise and epistemology.

A SHORT ESSAY ON EXPERTISE

It is fairly easy to accept at some level that citizens can invent new knowledge. But what is the relative value of this knowledge? Are they experts? In his introduction to Janice Lauer's recent book on invention, Charles Bazerman (2004) writes that any theory of invention is meant to answer fundamental questions. A writer's basic questions (e.g., what do I write about?)

> rest on even more fundamental philosophic questions about the nature of writing: What can we as individuals and communities know and claim? How do we know things and how might we share that knowledge with others? How can we represent what we know and believe and how does representation realize or transform our beliefs and knowledge? (xv)

What confounds the ability of most citizens to ask and answer the questions Bazerman posits is not just the tremendous technological, scientific, and institutional (bureaucratic) complexity that characterizes contemporary life, but also the commonplace understanding that knowledge is produced by outside experts and only *used* within communities. Experts and expertise, therefore, have a powerful practical as well as conceptual presence in communities and our larger understanding of who produces knowledge.

Many philosophers of science will trace the rise of expertise to the dramatic change in the status of science since the Enlightenment (e.g., Brown, 1998), and those concerned with understanding the concept of *expertise* will certainly touch on the role of the professions in protecting the power of experts, both economically and intellectually. Geisler (1994) writes, for example, that "it has become almost impossible to understand expertise independently of the unique social position garnered by modern professions" (p. 67), and Gaventa (1993) notes that expertise is like a club that requires degrees and certifications and grants rewards. Both perspectives on the power and growth of science and expertise are useful background for my concerns with contemporary, community-situated rhetorical practices. Thus, Irwin (1995) begins his book on "citizen science" by focusing on the role of science and questions of knowledge as they pertain to "competing notions of social progress" (pp. 6-7). In doing so, he reviews statements made over time by various English scientific bodies about the relationship between science and society, and specifically about the need for society to develop a "correct" understanding of science. Based on this review, Irwin develops a list of "notions" or assumptions that he attaches to how scientists and experts perceive themselves and (their relation to) society:

- the notion of contemporary "public ignorance" in matters of science and technology;
- the notion that a better understanding of science will lead to better "public and personal decisions";
- the notion that science is a force for human improvement;
- an explicit or implicit notion that science is itself value-free—although there are moral and political choices to be made about its *direction*;
- the notion that the life of citizens is somehow impoverished by an exclusion from scientific thought;
- the notion that wider exposure to scientific thinking will lead to greater acceptance and support for science and technology. (p. 14)

Irwin's argument is that these closely held assumptions prevent sound approaches to the most complex scientific and social problems facing human societies. The assumptions reveal, for Irwin, the pervasive view within the scientific establishment that they "get it" and the rest of us do not. Irwin believes that scientists and nonscientists alike have failed to understand the characteristics of a "risk society" and the ever closer weaving of the scientific and the social. Richard Harvey Brown (1998) is blunter in his assessment of the problem and clearer in terms of where he places the blame. Brown writes that expert decision makers and disciplines assume a public incapable of rational decision making. Expert disciplines and professions are therefore "successful in cultivating such civic incompetence to the extent that ordinary citizens come to regard, say, foreign policy or scientific research as remote from their own daily concerns" (p. 5). He continues: "Indeed, the technicist rhetoric of policy sciences explicitly eschews the deliberative rhetoric through which, since Aristotle, citizens were said to prudently conduct their civic life" (p. 5).

The concerns voiced by Brown and Irwin are richly revealed in case examples. Perhaps no text is more powerful in this regard than James Scott's (1998) *Seeing Like a State*, which chronicles the expert-driven planning practices of centralized political economies in the 20th century. Scott details truly catastrophic results and argues that these impacts could have been prevented or mitigated given attention to various forms of local knowledge. This argument is further reinforced by those working on "the development of indigenous knowledge," often in connection with development projects. As Sillitoe (1998) argues, based on his long-standing work in this area, "it is increasingly acknowledged . . . that other people have their own effective 'science' and resource use practices and that to assist them we need to understand something about their knowledge and management systems" (p. 223). The failure to develop such understandings—the outright blindnesses of expert institutions—can sometimes be absurd, as John Gaventa (1993) shows in this story:

> I have a friend, an activist, worker, and former coal miner who knows and loves the Appalachian mountains as well as anyone in my acquaintance. Over the last two decades, he has become a self-taught "expert" on the ravages that strip mining have gouged into the countryside. . . . His knowledge derives from vast experience and self-education, though it lacks the credentials that a degree or a government office might bring.
>
> One day, this friend asked the appropriate government inspector to file a complaint against what appeared to be a clear violation of the law. . . . My friend had discovered a major slide of silt running from a mine into a nearby stream on the mountain above his home, endangering the aquatic life and increasing the likelihood of flooding.
>
> The government inspector possessed a knowledge very different from that of my friend. A recent product of a state university, he was now a certified geologist. A junior post in a state regulatory agency helped to ordain his knowledge as "official." . . . Unlike my friend, his was the knowledge of expertise, not of experience.
>
> He accompanied my friend to inspect the mine on the basis of this expertise—as required by law. My friend showed him the silt oozing into the water. As also provided for by the law, he exercised his right as a citizen by asking the inspector to file a complaint against the responsible mining company. The expert official studied the situation. He drew out his maps and documents. And then he said, "I'm sorry, I cannot take action. According to my map, there is no stream there." (pp. 21-22)

Stories like this are almost too good (and awful) to be true. If they weren't true, we would have to invent them. But stories such as Gaventa's are true, although most of them are much more mundane. Such commonplace experiences are why Merrifield (1993) can write that increased citizen concern with environmental and health issues "have brought many people into confrontation with the scientific establishment and its values for the first time" (p. 66). And she, too, provides pointed case examples of citizens dismissed as "subjective" and "irrelevant" when pointing out that a landfill was literally poisoning them; scientists silenced or dismissed for asking the institutionally inappropriate questions; and the general difficulties citizens confront when trying to find good information, when trying to do their own science. This is the same dynamic I have experienced through citizens in Harbor. They, too, confront significant health and environmental threats. They also must confront institutions of expertise that deploy scientists whose purpose is to deliver a proper understanding of science. And they are often dismissed as "subjective" and for asking "irrelevant" questions.

Up to this point I have been pretty hard on "science" and "experts," and although I think there is every reason to be concerned about the arrogance and periodic violence done in the name of science by experts, how people experience complex situations in their own lives and their relationships with those individuals and institutions of expertise is highly variable. As Barbara, one of our key community contacts in Harbor, said to me about what they need from those of us from outside the community, "it is useful to have someone from a prestigious university stand up and say these are the facts." Too often, Barbara said, people from outside, particularly universities, "all want to come out and talk to us." What we need, she reminded me, is science.[2]

In my experience in Harbor and other communities, those from "outside" a given community who are working within that community—individuals and organizations who are present because of some expertise—are valued and welcomed because of their expertise and ability to do good science. I have yet to experience a situation in which "outsiders," "experts," and "science" have been rejected out of hand, although I know this happens. Rather, the dynamic is significantly more complex and nuanced. People working and writing within communities need help, and they know it. But they do not need certain kinds of help, as I have tried to highlight in this brief discussion. Much more importantly, people working together in communities are capable of writing their way to expertise. This is exactly the point of this chapter. Indeed, people in communities *must* invent their way to a place in public deliberation.

DOING SCIENCE IN HARBOR, LANSING, AND THROUGH THE INTERFACE: COORDINATED WRITING PROCESSES

One reason why the previous discussion is so important for me is that it illustrates why I have become deeply interested in how people can have a say in decisions that impact their lives. There is plenty of political philosophy that makes the case for why citizens should have a role to play—ethically, procedurally, legally (e.g., Benhabib, 2004; Habermas, 1993). The "expert" side of me finds this discussion compelling and relevant; the "nonexpert" side of me has experienced it as largely irrelevant. To be relevant, I have learned that people working for community change must be able to make something. They must invent. They must write. They must have a rhetoric, and it is a rhetoric that is inescapably technological in nature. The following examples of writing processes show success and failure, and they also show that "community literacies" are technological and coordinated (if not collaborative) in nature.

Harbor

As I wrote in chapter 3, I have been working for nearly two years now on a risk communication project in the community of Harbor, a city that has as much industrial density as any area in North America. In Harbor, there exists a short, man-made river channel that links various industrial operations with a lake. Periodically, this channel must be dredged to allow barge traffic. The sediments in the channel are heavily polluted, and these sediments currently flow into the lake, polluting that water body. For navigational and environmental reasons, the channel must be dredged. Dredging these sediments, however, creates another set of problems, as the dredging operation threatens to resuspend contaminants in the water. Furthermore, the transportation of the sediments creates risks, as does the disposal and treatment of the sediments.

As I also described in chapter 3, there are a number of powerful institutions involved in this project, which is one reason why the citizen groups participating in the decision-making processes associated with this project are at a considerable disadvantage. Despite the disadvantages, these citizen groups must act if they have any hope of directing the course of the deliberative process, and to engage effectively, they must create new knowledge about the issues at stake (and about the community). Here I review how one local organization, CEC, invents new knowledge and, in so doing, invents itself.

CEC is a loose collection of individuals, some with college degrees, some with degrees in relevant scientific disciplines, but most without either. Attendance at organizational meetings is typically twenty individuals, mostly women, with a race and ethnicity make up that varies slightly from the demography of the community (white members attend meetings at levels slightly higher than their presence in the community at large). Briefly, then, here is how that organization invents new knowledge:

1. At meetings, members are asked if they have knowledge or leads about the issue of concern.
2. Members read all relevant public documents about the issue of concern.
3. Members read widely in newspapers, magazines, and select scientific journals (e.g., *Nature*) for relevant articles.
4. Members write to experts cited in publications to ask follow-up questions or to ask these experts new questions based on the local situation.
5. Members report back at meetings about what has been discovered (and then return to searching and reading strategies).
6. Members write issue summaries for distribution to the wider community.

There is considerable complexity masked by this list, of course. But it suggests some things about how this organization writes. The first issue is that the rhetor in this process is not an individual. In fact, to study rhetorical practice in contemporary public forums is to abandon the study of individual writers because a focus on individual writers obscures the most important and complex rhetorical activity taking place. The inventional practices and communication activities that I observed in Harbor are fundamentally the acts of organizations. There are, obviously, individuals acting within these organizations, and indeed, there are varying levels of cooperation and collaboration. But this does not change the basic fact of distributed rhetorical activity and the necessity of understanding this distributed activity.

So what does this distributed activity look like? Figure 4.1 shows one representation of this distributed activity. Each box and corresponding letter represents an individual in the organization, their area of expertise, and the most visible interactions between them. Many of the interactions are visible in meetings, and the meeting is an important context for writing. At meetings there is a loose reporting procedure in which individuals report to the group on interesting and relevant things that they have read or found. This reporting then sometimes triggers discussion and some organ-

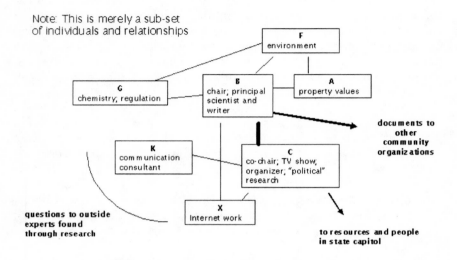

Note: This is merely a sub-set of individuals and relationships

Fig. 4.1. Distributed invention in Harbor

izing and action items. But as the map also shows, there are individuals in the organization who have their own specialties, and they tend to investigate and report on those issues both in CEC meetings and public meetings. The interactions that take place in meetings are important on their face, but there is also a deeper layer of activity that is not visible.

Two members of this organization conducted a neighborhood epidemiological survey (a household survey). Others in the organization actively monitor things like sewage discharge. But much of the work concerns searching and reading, both online and in more traditional ways. When we first asked Barbara (represented in Fig. 4.1 as "B") how she did her science, her answer was that she reads. It is not quite that simple. Barbara does not have reliable Internet access, nor does she use a computer very well. So her reading is largely newspaper, magazine, and journal based, although she manages to get her hands on a number of government and organizational reports from online sources. Other individuals in the organization and her family do networked-based searching and reading, and people help Barbara with whatever computer-based work she needs done.

Another layer of this distributed work is how the organization reads. Some readers read abstracts and summaries. Others go immediately to footnotes, references, and data sets. In this way, the distributed reading practices of CEC mirror the distributed reading expertise within corporate organizations. The reading and sharing then triggers another layer of activity, tracking down outside expertise. As Barbara told us once, "We couldn't do anything with what we know," so many individuals in this organization track down scientists or others whom they find through articles and news reports and whom they think can answer a question for them. They send questions, data sets, and documents. And from what we can tell, they get a high level of response to their inquiries. The organization is also capable of mining databases available over networks and those that are geographically isolated in places like the state capitol. They also maintain their own databases, such as financial records related to the city of Harbor, which is notoriously corrupt.

This coordinated rhetorical practice scales to more fine-grained practices as well. Consider the following document as an example (see Fig. 4.2). I have reproduced the first page of a four-page document in which CEC,

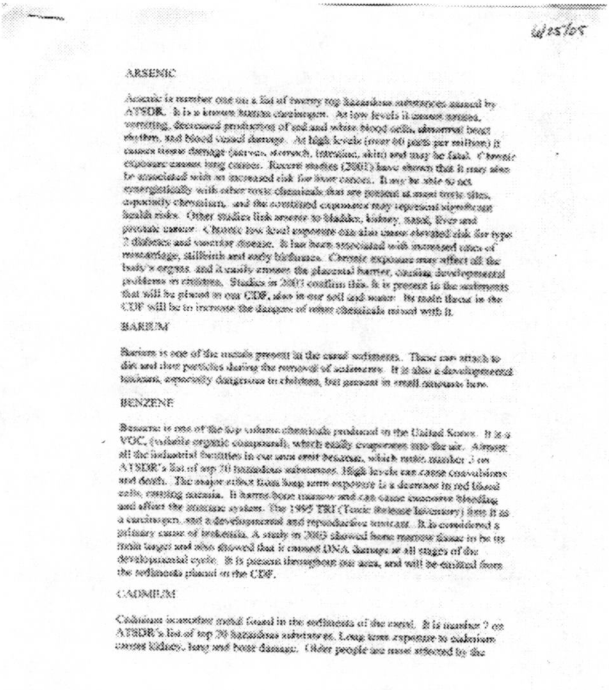

Fig. 4.2. Summary of chemicals written by CEC, Summer 2005

with Barbara as a lead writer, annotates thirteen chemicals and chemical compounds, followed by a summary. The summary notes that of the thirty-two compounds listed as important for the Harbor CDF by the Corps and EPA, CEC now has information on twenty-two of them. So this document only reports on a portion of the chemicals that they have researched. Of the twenty-two chemicals and compounds researched, CEC notes that ten are considered developmental toxicants, seven carcinogenic, and eight reproductive toxicants. Developmental impacts and environmental contributors to childhood disease are particularly important to CEC.

There are two interesting issues with respect to this summary. The first concerns how these summaries are used by CEC within the community. I noted in the third chapter that CEC was a key organization in a network of organizations, both community-based and not, in the Harbor area (see discussion around Fig. 3.1). CEC has a solid sense of the community and their audience, and we have come to rely on them in both respects. They know where they fit within the larger community, and their sense of place in the community has been confirmed to us by how others perceive CEC. They have a strong sense of who is a member of the community and who is not (this is, of course, an issue of some contention), and they seem to have developed a communication strategy designed to provide quality information to others in the community. Their communication practices also serve as an organizing tactic and a strategy that enables them to confront the Corps, EPA, and City at every opportunity. So, for example, they have developed and utilize a phone tree for communication; they distribute summaries and issue papers to individuals and other organizations, documents we know to be used by these other organizations; and they are always present and vocal in public meetings. That is, they understand the effective delivery networks within the community and use them. It was common for representatives of other organizations to say that they received scientific information from CEC—or from Barbara—and even to show us issue summaries just like the one represented in Figure 4.2. These summaries are a basic way that many individuals in Harbor learn about scientific and technical issues related to the dredging project. This science is distributed via a network of individuals and organizations, and therefore, it sustains connections between individuals and organizations.

The second issue has to do with how a document like this is written. The lead writer of this document is certainly Barbara. But she is not the only writer, and the organization is certainly its author (never are these summaries attributed to a single author; the design is always as generic as this document). But Barbara did not—and could not—write this alone. She first relied on the assistance of her daughter to help her get online and search the ToxFAQ database from the Agency for Toxic Substances and Disease Registry (a federal agency within Health and Human Services). She also accessed old (1992) Toxics Release Inventory data given to her by a local government official whose job is environmental monitoring and cleanup. She also accessed periodicals, like *Environmental Health Perspectives*, for information. Some of these periodicals Betty owns; others she gets from colleagues and the library. The composing process of this document mirrors the distributed work model represented in Figure 4.1, although it represents a more fine-grained level of activity. Just as importantly, the composing process relies on an infrastructure to support the knowledge work of writing. Figure 4.3 is an attempt to represent this distributed work and fragment of infrastructure. As I move through later chapters in the book, I continue to construct elements of infrastructure that are visible in the knowledge work of citizenship and therefore required for writing in communities.

As one looks at Figure 4.3, there are a number of features to notice. The first is the elements of infrastructure that support the work of writing a document: computers, computer networks, interfaces, databases, chairs, desks, paper, pens, people, and so on. Then there are the elements of infrastructure that connect to what I discussed in chapter 2—the federal data

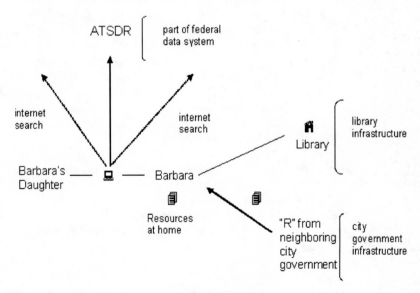

Fig. 4.2. Distributed work and infrastructures supporting the writing of a document

system in particular—but also elements of more local infrastructures, such as the resources of a local public library or city government.[3] Even at the level of a relatively simple 4-page document, the activity required is complex, as are the technologies necessary for writing and the infrastructure required to support such knowledge work. When we move again to think of infrastructure at an organizational level, elements like software, telephone lines, workspace, and meeting places become increasingly important, but so do human networks, issues of culture, and connections to more macro infrastructural resources. The writing done in Harbor to enact community change is impossible without the infrastructure to support it.

Troubled Interfaces

As I described it in chapter 3, the Capital Area Community Information (CACI) project is an example of a "community informatics" project and also an attempt to both understand and make infrastructure. It is a project focused on designing with "users" (citizens) information communication technologies that will support their knowledge work in communities. CACI is a study of an existing informatics effort called CACVoices (http://www.cacvocies.org), and it includes both the public website that hosts databases and other types of public information and the community organizations that contribute to and rely on that resource (see Fig. 3.2 for a look at a typical welcome screen for CACVoices). Like many data-rich interfaces, CACVoices provides an array of options couched in expert languages, but it is intended for nonexpert users. The problems suggested by these interfaces are substantial, both at the interface (usability) and in terms of their implications for what users can do with the information (usefulness). Here I describe use through (and around) this articulation of tools. The discussion focuses on basic usability problems and how those problems surface failures of the infrastructure necessary to support the knowledge work of citizens in communities. My intent is a fine-grained look at relationships between technological infrastructure and invention.

According to the study design that I also provided in the third chapter, year one of the CACI project was to establish baseline data on local information technology capacity and use and identify usability problems with CACVoices. This was indeed our focus during year one, but the first task, which I do not detail here, was to build relationships with users of CACVoices, people who work for social service agencies in Lansing, who work for community-based organizations, or who volunteer with similar organizations. These people are busy, of course, and so we spent nearly a year just talking to them. In study design language, we called that talking an "interview," and indeed, we designed these initial conversations to get at certain issues, such as the experiences of users interacting with CACVoices and their sense of usability problems.

Based on our analysis of these interviews, we developed use scenarios that were both consistent with typical user activity and would push hard on potential usability problems that we thought our initial analysis had identified. These potential usability problems, although mundane in nature, were serious impediments to day-to-day use of this set of advanced ICTs for invention and writing. Utilizing Michigan State University's Usability and Accessibility Center (http://usability.msu.edu/), we then asked some of those we interviewed to participate in a standard usability evaluation. This evaluation was conducted June 20-23, 2005. The website was evaluated in one-on-one usability sessions with ten participants, including five regular users of the site and five "power" users, who had previously undergone training for designing web pages on the CACVoices site.[4] The evaluation was designed to answer the following questions:

- What do users like and dislike about the CACVoices website?
- What aspects of the CACVoices website are hard to use?
- What are user expectations regarding the site organization (e.g., navigation, number of levels, organization of content, etc.)?

The one-on-one sessions lasted one-and-a-half hours for each participant and included several components:

- Verbal overview description of study—Participants were given a description of the general nature of the study, and the order of activities that will be included in the session.
- Informed consent form for human subjects—Each participant was asked to sign the Consent Form before they could participate in the study.
- Demographic questionnaire—We administered a questionnaire to gather background information on participants' work experience and Internet experience.
- Background interview—We then spent about five minutes of the session identifying participants' typical work activities and procedures and discussing the situations during which they might interact with the CACVoices website or use the transit system.
- Task scenarios performance—Participants were asked to perform several task scenarios using the CACVoices website, find-

ing general and specific information on the website.
Participants were asked to think aloud, verbalizing any confusion while performing tasks, to identify areas of difficulty, as
well as patterns and types of participant errors when performing typical search tasks.

- Poststudy questionnaire—A poststudy questionnaire was
  administered to address specific aspects of the task scenarios
  and obtain satisfaction ratings.

Participants were also debriefed at the end of the session to capture any
final thoughts. The metrics used to assess the evaluation were typical for
usability evaluations of this kind. Key usability goals included effectiveness,
which refers to how well a system does what it is supposed to do; efficiency, or the way a system supports users in carrying out their tasks; and satisfaction, which relates to the subjective responses users have to the system. The usability performance measures included:

- percentage of tasks completed successfully
- number and types of errors
- mean time to perform a particular task
- mean number of web page changes

The qualitative measures included:

- feedback from the pretest interview
- user satisfaction ratings (poststudy questionnaire)
- verbal feedback during and after the session
- written feedback on the demographic and poststudy question-
  naires

Evaluations were video and audiotaped, and at least two people were
observing and taking notes for each evaluation (we sometimes had a third
researcher with us).

Overall, users were quite successful in locating certain information
within the CACVoices website, such as a specific phone number or posting
a forum message. However, users had a more difficult time understanding
the site's presentation of information pertaining to data and mapping, as
well as organizational issues, such as when information was not located in
the area of the site where they expected it to be. In other words, the deeper a user needed to go into the site or the more complex the interfaces that
were required, the more difficult tasks became. Failure and frustration rose

accordingly. In general, then, some unsurprising but critical usability problems were identified. The current site is not accessible; it does not meet Section 508 standards and Priority 1 guidelines of the Web Content Accessibility Guidelines. In addition, the navigation of the site presents significant conceptual and, therefore, functional problems, due to the fact that there are multiple navigation tools (redundancy is a problem in this case) and the categorization and language of the navigation is opaque even to users who are experienced. Related to these navigational problems is the fact that what information designers would call "content" or "information types" are consistently mismatched, leading both to confusion as to the purpose of a given page in the site and the need to find related information on multiple pages. Then there is the need to make the visual treatment and page design functionality similar across all pages and reduce the number of graphical and color elements on the page to ensure that users notice the text and links embedded within them (users overlooked graphics and colored areas because they were perceived as nonessential or advertisements). An effective search functionality is missing but necessary.

To those experienced in usability or web design, the issues I have identified here seem obvious. In themselves, they add little, if anything, to the research or scholarly literature on usability or web design. I spend the time detailing them because despite the fact that we identified problems that were arguably predictable and, therefore, should have been solved, these were problems that were, in fact, not predicted and not solved. I am claiming, therefore, that basic usability problems and the work necessary to address them is not obvious and is more of a problem in community settings than one might otherwise think. Corporate organizations using networked writing technologies to make money *may* devote the resources to solve usability problems. But what about governments or community organizations themselves? If they had the resources, would they spend in them in this way? I'm not so sure. And the fundamental reason for this is the pervasive view that access to information is by itself good, particularly in community settings where access to information technologies has been a long and hard-fought battle. More powerful institutions have moved on to problems of knowledge work, effective use, and what I call here "invention." That has not been the case with less powerful institutions and communities.

In my experience with community computing projects, urban planning may be the most significant locus for ICT applications, primarily through the deployment of GIS tools (sometimes called PPGIS, or Public Participation Geographic Information Systems). As Harrison and Haklay (2002) characterize it, the goals of PPGIS include "the use of GIS by grassroots communities to improve their purchase on the public debate" and the drive to increase public participation in decision making (p. 841). Given this, there is some concern for providing useful, interactive systems that both permit access to databases and enable citizens and local groups to create new data and information. But as Ghose (2001) writes, the same technologies that make it possible to provide data access to communities, by virtue of their cost and complexity, are fundamentally elitist and there-fore often inaccessible. What is remarkable in the planning literature as it pertains to technology access is the *invisibility* of the users of advanced information technologies (e.g., Tulloch & Shapiro, 2003). In the Craig, Harris, and Weiner (2002) collection, *actual use* of PPGIS by its intended audience is absent (see Ferreira, 1999; Shaw & Shaw, 1999, for cases of success). Only Kingston (2002) notes that professionals were more com-mon and successful users of computers and public database tools than nonprofessionals. Indeed, in many of the studies discussed in the Craig, Harris, and Weiner collection, problems of use are indirectly addressed by the use of community workshops and ongoing intermediary support. In this approach to the problem, university experts walk community leaders through a demonstration of how the tools work, record the successes, and are comfortable that the technology and information has transferred. Planners assume that because these technologies are available and useful to experts, they easily transfer to different contexts and users and lead to greater institutional efficiency and public participation (e.g., Smith & Massimo, 2003).⁵

My conclusion is that basic usability issues are often invisible in the very projects designed to expand access. As we have learned in the CACI project, however, these basic usability issues prevent use. They short-circuit public participation and citizen activism. They disable invention. This fail-ure is even more visible if we look at more complex inventional work through advanced information technologies. In our evaluation we asked users to map burglaries in a specific area and locate and use a data table with information about smoking rates (common tasks with often used databases). These tasks were the most difficult in the evaluation. Only three of ten users were able to map the burglary data, and on average it took them nearly six minutes to do so. Finding the data table—which meant understanding the data in order to know that the right information had indeed been found—was only completed successfully by one user. The average time spent was two minutes and thirty-two seconds because users quit this task more quickly than the mapping task (see chapter 1 for a dis-cussion of writing that references similar data tables within CACVoices).

If one reflects back on the inventional practices in Harbor—or forward to the next section on the Allen Neighborhood Center—then the technologically mediated inventional practices of citizen knowledge work are clearly dependent on basic interface activity. But take a look at the complexity of the interfaces provided to users. In Figure 4.4, we see the basic interface of a GIS application, with tools along the top and a layer control legend along the right. The left contains some help information, information that proved useful to users. Along the top right ("choose a map") is the place where users must go to start using the tool. The ability to launch the tool—to choose a map—proved to be the first problem for many users. The annotations in Figure 4.5 show where on the interface activity was required and the difficulties users encountered. At this level of the interface, however, many users were still successful. That is, they were able to map burglaries, ignore the legend, and pan and zoom effectively after trial and error. Once users got to layer three in the interface and the key interpretive task of locating specific crimes in a precise geographical area, things began to fall apart. The annotations in Figure 4.6 show the exact problems users had with the interface. They had trouble with spatial location, which was the key interpretive task of the scenario. That is, in order for the data to make sense—in order for the information to be useable in a report or a letter or a grant proposal—users need to have confidence that they are able to

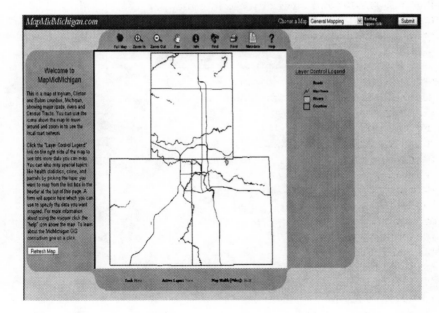

Fig. 4.4 Opening map interface

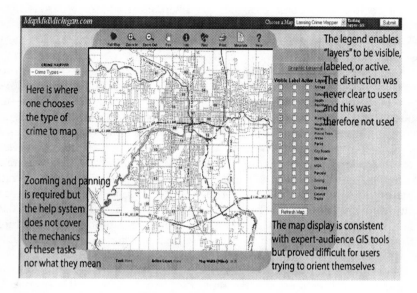

Fig. 4.5. The second layer of the crime mapper

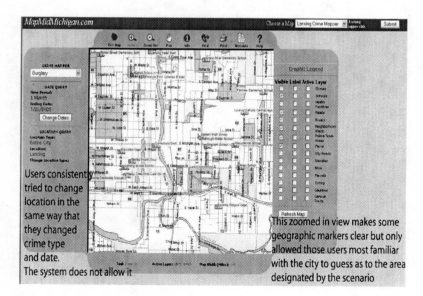

Fig. 4.6. Layer three of the mapping interface

locate data points in space. This is, after all, the point of a geographic information system. Without the confidence that they have information that is true, this inventional task is relatively useless. This proved to be the case with users. We asked them to tell us when they felt they completed the task successfully, and although most users got to the screen shown in Figure 4.6, few had confidence in the results of their search. The failure of the technologies to support user work is certainly the opacity of the system, but there is also a deeper failure of interpretation, a key and complex knowledge-making process that is also not well supported. In a usability evaluation, we could only identify relatively simple problems. We did not spend any time observing or working with people as they worked with the data. We didn't ask them to interpret the data in any significant way or fold it into an argument. Technologically, we didn't ask them to capture images from the interface, edit them, and incorporate them into another piece of writing as I have done here. We only saw the tip of the iceberg. Imagine, then, the scale of the inventional problems given the need to write with and through these technologies.

Allen Neighborhood Center

I turn now to a discussion of one community organization in Lansing, an organization that is a user of CACVoices.org and so part of the CACI study. The first two cases in this chapter focused on more particular inventional practices and their relationships to supporting infrastructures. With this look at the Allen Neighborhood Center, I want to zoom out a bit and look at strategic, highly organized knowledge work in communities and the problem of the lack of infrastructure for sharing that knowledge work with others.

The Allen Neighborhood Center (ANC) "serves as a hub for neighborhood education and capacity building," offering support for organized neighborhood groups, information and referral services, and a range of community building and healthy community activities on the eastside of Lansing, Michigan (see http://www.allenneighborhoodcenter.org for more information).[6] Over time, we have placed a professional writing intern at the Center, and I have worked with people from the Center on a handful of local initiatives. After my first meeting with people from ANC, I thought it was perhaps the most sophisticated and highly functional community-based organization I had ever seen. It is probably one of the smartest organizations I have ever seen in *any* context. So I return to ANC as another example illustrating knowledge work in communities.

The Allen Neighborhood Center has learned to work in a structured, inquiry-driven fashion. This was immediately obvious to me as an outsider, and the structure of their knowledge work was made more visible to me once I sat down to talk with the ANC director, Joan Nelson. As she told me, "we have always been consumers of data . . . most of us really believe that our strategies and ideas for addressing a whole array of issues need to be grounded in data. In fact. In information that is sound." This belief animates how they approach problem solving. In a typical project, the first piece is really the data-gathering piece. A project begins with an assessment of capacities, strengths, and needs in the neighborhood by holding focus groups, going to local meetings, and so on. That research process involves looking at whatever data might be available about the neighborhood with respect to particular issues (e.g., data from CACVoices or other government resources). They will also often collect their own data about the community to consider along with existing data (see Fig. 4.7 for a sample health survey instrument used for door-to-door surveys). Importantly, they began collecting their own data because there was a real need to do so. In ANC's view, the data available from outside the neighborhood (about the neighborhood) wasn't good enough. They needed information that was timely and scale appropriate. In other words, they didn't have time to wait for some statistical partners to produce data. And even then, some of the data is not scaled appropriately (e.g., census tract data is available but they need block-level data). They needed, therefore, to generate their own data at an appropriate scale and in a time frame sensitive to local conditions.

The door-to-door surveying, which they do regularly, is a key inquiry process and constitutes perhaps the heart of their expertise as an organization. The health team, for instance, knocks on doors each week to collect data and engage in conversation. The conversation is critical. Not only are they able to collect iterative quantitative data about the neighborhood, but through the surveys ANC is able to engage in a similarly structured listening process. This regular listening practice is deeply meaningful in terms of developing and maintaining relationships in the community, which I see as its primary value. That they also gather critical information is important too. In addition to the listening and conversation enabled by the door-to-door surveying, the ANC also has a set of advisory boards associated with each program in which neighborhood residents make up at least half the membership. They also hold a regular forum in the neighborhood. And as mentioned, focus groups are a common method within their research process.

As a source of knowledge and expertise, this research/problem-solving process is quite powerful. Joan Nelson described it to me as an iterative

---

Date: **Health Assessment 2004**   **Health Team Member:**

Name: Address: Rent or Own   Phone#:

Household composition: Number of children (ages):
                        Number of adults:

Health coverage

- 1. Do you have health coverage? Yes____ No____
    IHP
    Medicaid
    Private Pay Insurance
    Employer Pay Insurance
    Other

- 2. How would you rate your health?____ Poor _____Fair _____Good _____Excellent

3. Are you interested in finding out if you qualify for Medicaid or the Ingham Health Plan? Yes___ No___

    Have you applied for Ingham Health Plan or Medicaid in the past? Yes___ No___ When_____

    Is your annual income less than:
        $9,310
        $23,275
        $31,225
        $39,175
        $47,125

    Do you live in Ingham County? Yes___ No___

    How many people do you claim as dependents? No.____

    Do you have any other health coverage at all? Yes____ No____

- 4. Do you have prescription coverage? Yes___ No___
- 5. Do you have an established a health care provider?
- 6. Is there anyone in your household that does not have health coverage?

7. Would you like us to contact them regarding the Ingham Health Plan or Medicaid? Yes___ No___
    Name_____

Breast Health

- 1. Do you do a monthly breast self-exam? Yes____ No____ Why not?
- 2. Would a monthly reminder phone call/ postcard to do monthly self-exams be helpful? Yes___ No___
- 3. Have you ever had a clinical breast exam by a doctor or a nurse practitioner? Yes___ No___ Why not?

4. When was your last clinical breast exam by a doctor or a nurse practitioner?

- 5. Have you ever had a mammogram? Yes___ No___ Why not?

8/24/2005   1

Fig. 4.7. Sample page from ANC Neighborhood Health Survey

process such that the inquiry is not a discrete phase that ends at a certain point in the process, as when they move to implement solutions. Rather, they are able to build a simple picture of the neighborhood with respect to a particular issue rather quickly by accessing local, state, and federal data systems.[7] This constitutes one "layer" of the map they build. To this layer they add their own data, which tells certain stories and reveals particular patterns. To these layers they then add the "qualitative data"—the stories—

for essential richness and complexity. The result, as Joan told me, is that "we are able in these very practical ways to learn new things, confirm what we expect, and actually challenge the assumptions we are carrying."

As one can imagine, the infrastructure necessary to conduct this work is significant. ANC coordinates with twenty funders, so grant writing and management are key writing and infrastructural issues. They work very hard on information systems integration across projects, but this is hampered by the fact that they run almost exclusively on donated or otherwise older technologies and little human support for this work. There is no information systems department within a community-based organization. To do much of their writing work, they use common Microsoft Office packages, but they also regularly generate their own spreadsheets and Access databases. The writing of these databases is a common organizational function. As Joan asserted, "the potential around data . . . we still have so far to go. We are not fully exploiting and understanding the data we do have." They are making significant strides to create and write the databases that will enable them to more fully use the information they regularly collect. As I have shown earlier in this chapter, accessing existing local, state, and federal data systems is not easy to do, and so ANC has had to develop the expertise to effectively query databases and work on computer networks. To create data maps, they must have people who use ArcView, a GIS package, and also people who can work with new media technologies, as their communication strategies are increasingly media rich.

It is possible to see, I think, why I find this organization to be so interesting. They are a knowledge organization. They simply function in a different context than is typical for a "knowledge organization," and they understand their work to be focused on outcomes other than "efficiency," "expediency," or profit maximization. Asked to articulate ANC's expertise, Joan said that they were good at comprehensive and integrated community development, and at identifying priority concerns and figuring out how to address them with the community. For Joan and ANC, the neighborhood is the next larger unit above family, and for them it is the most underutilized unit in the social structure for helping to solve problems. And ANC makes a difference. The health program is signing up people in significant numbers for the county health insurance plan; people in the neighborhood regularly give up smoking; and new health-related groups spring up in the neighborhood regularly. But let me close this section with a précis of their food security program. As part of their regular community surveying a few years ago, ANC asked the U.S. Department of Agriculture's standard questions to gauge food security/insecurity (which means, roughly, access to nutritious, healthful diets). What they learned was stunning. They found that nearly 30% of the neighborhood was food insecure. This is a significant and serious impediment to general health and well being in a community.

As Joan suggested to me, the obvious solution was more and bigger food pantries. When people do not have enough to eat, then it is necessary to feed them. ANC, as part of their inquiry process, decided first to do just the opposite. They actually capped the size of their existing food pantry. In conjunction with this, they immediately focused on understanding where people shopped, what types of food were available at these stores and their cost, and finally, what the barriers were to access to more and better food (issues such as money, store locations, quality of food available). In conjunction with local farmers and other partners, they began enabling fresh produce to be brought into the community and, quickly building on that, started a farmers market as a way to increase access to high-quality products, with the added effect of creating a market for local farmers. The goal of this project is food self-reliance and sustainability, and the next phase includes projects like hoop houses and community gardens. The goal is to become the center for urban agriculture in the city of Lansing, a place where local residents are food secure and that generates new business, capital, and capacity in the community. When Joan tells me that ANC has been pretty good at figuring out the neighborhood piece of solutions to complex problems, she is identifying their area of expertise as citizens in the Lansing community. What should not be missed as part of this expertise is the status of ANC as a knowledge-maker. They have embedded inquiry into all of their functions, and they make the knowledge they produce a regular part of their communication strategy, whether in a community meeting or a grant proposal. One significant limitation of the work of organizations like ANC is their ability to share knowledge. Note that one reason they must make new knowledge is the fact that existing databases, like those found on CACVoices, are insufficient. But are community-created databases found on CACVoices? Are they sharing what they learn with other community organizations? Are they a networked part of a local information infrastructure? This is unclear, and it is to this issue that I turn in the fifth chapter.

TOWARD A *techne* OF COMMUNITY KNOWLEDGE WORK

I have shown in this chapter what I understand to be the most important features of invention in communities. Those who write in communities to create change write through and with a range of advanced information technologies. This is required of even the smallest and least structured organizations, in large part because of the need to demonstrate expertise to public audiences. Writing in communities is coordinated work (and sometimes collaborative). This work is distributed within an organization and sometimes across organizations. This, too, is necessary because of the complexity of working and writing in communities. These two basic insights have significant implications for what is needed to support community work and organizations, an issue I take up in the next chapter, and I believe there are equally significant implications for how we teach writing in schools, which I take up in the last chapter.

I focus on the concept of *invention* because there are epistemological issues at stake in the work that takes place in communities. I have used the concept of "knowledge work" not precisely because it evokes a type of distributed, technology-intensive work, but because knowledge matters so deeply to how and why the less powerful can be persuasive.[8] Making visible and usable local knowledge is essential in any complex endeavor. As Scott (1998) argues, complex social activities have often relied on a thin veneer of "scientific" planning and so are driven by a "necessarily thin, schematic model of social organization and production animating the planning . . ." (p. 310). Often ignored or suppressed are the practical skills that "underwrite any complex activity" (p. 311). Scott continues:

> The point that I am making would hardly need emphasis or elaborate illustration except for the fact that a certain understanding of science, modernity, and development has so successfully structured the dominant discourse that all other kinds of knowledge are regarded as backward, static traditions, as old wives' tales and superstitions. High modernism has needed this "other," this dark twin, in order to rhetorically present itself as the antidote to backwardness. The binary opposition also comes from a history of competition between the institutions and personnel that sprang up around these two forms of knowledge. Modern research institutions, agricultural experiment stations, sellers of fertilizer and machinery, high-modernist city planners, Third World developers, and World Bank officials have, to a considerable degree, made their successful institutional way in the world by the systematic denigration of the practical knowledge that we have called *metis*. (pp. 331-332)

Metis, then, is a form of local knowledge that Scott equates with know-how, experience, or knack—knowledge embedded in local experience (see also Johnson, 1998). He writes that *metis* "represents a wide array of practical skills and acquired intelligence in responding to a constantly changing natural and human environment" (p. 313). It is generally the ability to adapt and to understand. And *metis* is local, a function of practice, and in some of Scott's characterizations, almost innate. He writes: "In a sense, metis lies in that large space between the realm of genius, to which no formula can apply, and the realm of codified knowledge, which can be learned by rote" (p. 316). Naming and understanding this form of knowledge is critical to Scott's argument, for both the knowledge of expert institutions and local knowledges are necessary for complex work to be completed successfully, particularly for those less powerful. In a similar way, this form of local knowledge is critical for my argument, and certainly for those illustrated in this chapter. Invention matters.

There are a number of systematic inventional practices that emerge from the examples in this chapter. The first is reading. Finding and understanding a "literature," as Agre (1995) would understand it, is an important issue. There are two additional issues associated with this reading practice. One is the distributed nature of reading. Within CEC and ANC, there are individuals with specific reading interests and abilities that enable them to process some literatures in ways experts would process them. The second issue is what effective reading and networked communication technologies enable: the ability to contact outside experts with good questions and maintain relationships with these experts. In both Harbor and Lansing, we also see organizations that conduct door-to-door surveys focused on health data. The particular focus isn't as interesting as the practice itself. Two sources of expertise flow from this practice as well, the ability to collect data that is not collected by other organizations and the structured listening moments that the research practice enables. Finally, there is the issue of mining and making databases. I hope that I have shown that access to public databases is still a very serious problem. In fact, I would submit that the problem is growing more severe, not less so. Increasingly because of government policy and technological capacity, more and more specialist information technologies are pushed into communities and civic life without the necessary support for the work of nonspecialist users. Thus, the ability to access and mine relatively simple databases is quite complex, and organizations that have developed that capacity are more highly functional than those that have not. Perhaps surprising is the number of organizations who make and maintain databases. This writing practice cannot be overlooked, as it is fundamental to the knowledge work of citizenship and enables other writing practices. Through this work, then, the expertise in communities is visible. *Metis* can be captured and made visible.

From the examples in this chapter, it is also possible to see actual writing processes and the outlines of a rhetoric that is useful to citizens in situations of technical, scientific, and institutional complexity. That rhetoric is rooted in an epistemology that values *metis* and local expertise, requires the technologies and infrastructure to support knowledge-making practices, and therefore is focused on transformative and transgressive possibility. Why must civic rhetoric be animated by these commitments? Because those in positions of structured inequality—I have called them "citizens"—can make things—arguments, documents, media—that enable reversals in particular places and at specific times. That is, this rhetoric must rise to the level of what Atwill (1998) would call a *techne, the Greek concept* of art that has been at the center of historical discussions of rhetorical pedagogy and practice for a very long time. Atwill traces the concept of *techne* back to the *Odyssey*, where it signified both implement and boundary, prompting her interpretation that "the accomplishments of art are, paradoxically, tied to its boundaries" (p. 47). She explains that whenever a boundary or limit was recognized, art created a path that transgressed and redefined the boundary. Outlining the ancient conceptions of *techne*, she offers the following:

> 1) A *techne* is never a static normative body of knowledge. It may be described as a *dynamis* (or power), transferable guides and strategies, a cunningly conceived plan—even a trick or a trap. This knowledge is stable enough to be taught and transferred but flexible enough to be adapted to particular situations and purposes.
>
> 2) A *techne* resists identification with a normative subject. The subjects identified with *techne* are often in a state of flux or transformation. [. . .] Since a *techne* is always transferable, no matter how brilliant the plan or strategy, it is never confined to a specific human or god. In other words, *techne* is never "private" knowledge, a mysterious faculty, or the product of unique genius.
>
> 3) *Techne* marks a domain of intervention and invention. A *techne* is *never* knowledge as representation. *Techne* appears when one is outnumbered by foes or overpowered by force. It not only enables the transgression of boundaries but also attempts to *rectify* transgressions. (p. 48)

Atwill explains that in the mythic traditions of the Prometheus accounts, *techne* is depicted as a trick, contrivance, or stratagem, as well as a method of making or doing that is set against nature (*physis*) and force (*bia*). Techne is a uniquely temporal and situated kind of knowledge. In discussing the relationship between *techne* and *kairos*, for example, Atwill points out that "knowing how" and "knowing when" to deploy an art distinguishes *techne* from "rule-governed activities that are less constrained by temporal conditions" (p. 59). She further argues that ancient conceptions of *techne* are identified with cunning intelligence (*metis*), not practical wisdom (*phronesis*). Thus, *techne* becomes subversive, a way of inventing knowledge and persuasive discourse that seeks to counter domination. Is there a techne of/for citizen (civic) rhetorical practice? Do we see this in the work of community organizations in this chapter?

I think so. I think we see a resistance to static and normative bodies of knowledge in people's efforts to create counter-knowledges and communication tools that enable resistance and change. The distributed nature of the work illustrated in these examples speaks to the requirement to teach to others the habits and practices of a given organization and transfer as much expertise as possible across networks of people and activity. And the rhetorical activity of these organizations has certainly enabled outright resistance and more commonplace change initiatives. Would this activity be possible without an effective rhetoric? I am not so sure. What I am sure of, however, is that effective knowledge work in communities is not a simple function of individual capacity or effective project teams. It requires an infrastructure, and I turn to the design of that infrastructure in the next chapter.

NOTES

1. I am using Lauer's (2004) understanding of invention in this book: "The term *invention* has historically encompassed strategic acts that provide the discourser with direction, multiple ideas, subject matter, arguments, insights or probable judgments, and understanding of the rhetorical situation. Such acts include initiating discourse, exploring alternatives, framing and testing judgments, interpreting texts, and analyzing audiences" (p. 2).

2. All names of individuals, locations, and organizations are pseudonyms. All quotations come from fieldnotes.

3. There are always elements of local information infrastructures that are not necessarily part of a wider information infrastructure. In Harbor, for instance, there exists a local repository of documents related to the current dredging project, as well as other environmental projects. This document archive is unique to that area.

4. Participants indicated that they use the Internet at least two hours per week, usually every day, to check e-mail, check weather, chat/Instant Message, con-

duct research on various topics, play games, plan a trip or find a map, play or download music, online banking, find financial information, and/or shop online.

5.   Likewise, much of the digital government work that has been completed in the United States has understandably been concerned with policy (the focus of the National Center for Digital Government at Harvard) and making tools: portals, databases, data visualization systems, knowledge or content management architectures, systems for collaboration and decision making, and so on (e.g., Ambite et. al., 2001; Goddard et. al., 2003; McIver & Elmagarmid, 2002). Less consistent has been how digital government projects have been evaluated. Most common are survey-based evaluations of use and indicator-driven analyses of e-government portals that assess the presence of specific tools and functionality (e.g., Esterling, Lazer, & Neblo, 2004; or the work of Cyber State in Michigan—http://www.cyber-state.org). Both approaches provide broad snapshots of e-government projects and use, and such breadth is useful in telling us what tools are available. It is less clear how often researchers have been interested in usability or usefulness or—most importantly—have understood these concepts and practices to be fundamental to the success of digital government. Becker's work (e.g., 2004a, 2004b) focusing on web accessibility for older adults is one important exception, and others have been concerned with actual use within the contexts of tool-focused projects (e.g., Dominick et al., 2003; Harrison & Zappen, 2003; Marchionini & Mu, 2003). It is still surprising that such evaluations are not more common and, in my view, that they are not foregrounded. That is, that usability and usefulness aren't driving factors in researching how to understand complex systems that are used by nonexperts as part of day-to-day activity.

6.   Allen Neighborhood Center is the real name of this organization, and the names of individuals associated with ANC are also real, at their request.

7.   The "they" invoked here is, of course, a fluid team that coordinates the work of a project. Because I showed the structure of one such team in Harbor, I do not create similar maps here. Each project will have a core team of 2-3 people who will work on a project consistently over time. Anywhere from 1-5 additional people will float into a project depending on the phase. Participating as well are advisory groups, both formal and informal, and some outside experts. The coordinated work at the ANC is more structured and managed than with CEC, but the pattern should be clear. The knowledge work of citizenship is fundamentally writing and communicative work, and that work is always coordinated if not collaborative in nature.

8.   I have not been explicit in this chapter—and will not be in this book—in my discussion of the audiences for these community organizations and how (indeed, if) they are persuasive. This is an exceedingly complex issue, in part because it is difficult to see as a researcher. I have seen the effectiveness of CEC's writing with other community organizations. Their understanding of science becomes "the community's" understanding fairly often. And this

organization—and others—have delayed a project for decades through their ability to communicate their opposition. ANC has been successful both within the community in facilitating change and with outside funders in acquiring resources. And this only touches on two types of audiences.

5

MAKING INFRASTRUCTURES
TO SUPPORT INVENTION

I am sitting in a bland, featureless meeting room with too little light and oxygen, listening to an academic presentation (complete with PowerPoint), praying for it to end. The speaker, though extremely well qualified and informed, has delivered a long, very dry discussion with little apparent attention to audience. Although *my* audience might imagine that I am listening to a presentation at an academic conference, I am actually in Harbor, on the evening of June 17, 2003, in a city council meeting room. The speaker, a scientist for the U.S. Army Corps of Engineers, seems motivated by an honest impulse to educate and inform. Toward that end, he provided a richly detailed, hour-long lesson on Confined Disposal Facilities.

The audience responded with anger. The government body that called the meeting was frustrated by the time taken for the presentation. Some community members, including Barbara, saw the presentation as a deliberate strategy to prevent public input. By speaking for more than an hour, the Corps effectively cut short the time available for other activities, such as questions from the community. As Barbara told me later that night, the presentation "told us everything we knew and nothing that we didn't know."

Enduring a meeting like this is not a common experience for me. Unfortunately for folks in Harbor, they often receive information critical to the dredging project in this way. As I discuss next, citizens across the United States also commonly receive "expert" information relevant to their communities in such a way. Was Barbara correct in reading the strategy as malignant? Perhaps. It might also be that the engineer's theory of audience and methods of delivery are flawed. The question that emerged for me in thinking of the meeting as infrastructure is this: Is the public meeting an end or a beginning?

*   *   *

I am sitting in my university's Usability and Accessibility Center watching our evaluation of the usability of CACVoices. I am watching a sophisticated user of CACVoices reason her way through some challenging interfaces and database tools. She has experience using databases, and so she persists trying to use this database. At the time, I thought her persistence was remarkable. In looking at the video later, I am even more struck by the sophistication of the activity we captured (see the video at http://www.wide.msu.edu/ccc/civic).

The user has a significant amount of experience and expertise in the domain of activity under consideration. She also easily recognizes the logic and structure of the query interface and the data table returned to her (she was almost unique in our user group in both regards). Given that, however, she has considerable difficulty and must reason her way through the interface. Yet even in her confusion, she is productive. She concludes that the presentation of data violates her expectations and that certain data variables presented to her are worthless. She also pulls together an interpretive narrative at the end. But she has little confidence in either the tool or the strength of her interpretation. She told us, for example, as a response to a post-task question, that she did not feel successful in completing the task asked of her. She makes new knowledge as part of this activity but doubts its usefulness.

*   *   *

These stories have something important in common. Both stories identify the problem space of invention in communities and foreground infrastructure as the missing element necessary to support invention. That is, the "problem" of invention in both cases is, at least in part, the lack of an infrastructure to support invention. My purpose in this chapter is to revisit the concept of infrastructure that I unpacked in chapter 2, with the goal of describing the creation of new infrastructures to support invention in communities. This chapter, therefore, is about the "action" component of an action research strategy. The action or intervention in each case is to make infrastructures with people in communities that support their ability to invent and write for community change.

INFRASTRUCTURES AND/AS *METIS* CAPABLE INSTITUTIONS

The example interventions that I discuss in this chapter are a new meeting and reporting process as part of the TOSC work in Harbor and a new mapping tool that we are using in Lansing. Before I get to those examples, I want to lay out a conceptual framework that I think is necessary for understanding the power of making infrastructures with others. Indeed, this framework is necessary for understanding the examples themselves. The framework is built on the following claim: people's ability to write for change in communities—particularly in relatively powerless communities—requires the development of "metis capable infrastructures" to support knowledge work.

One purpose of my work with the concept of "infrastructure" in the second chapter was to map, in the most general way, the infrastructures of community information. The concept of *infrastructure* has more than descriptive power. I am attracted to its design possibilities and its related ability to force us to reconsider how we understand the scenes of writing. Conceptually, then, there are a number of issues to recall from Star and Ruhleder's (1996) introduction of the concept. The first is the need to ask *when* an infrastructure is, not what it is. The value of this imperative is that it focuses our attention on activity, not on things. In this way, infrastructure is also embedded, learned, conventional, and often standardized (both technically and culturally). In addition, previous work on infrastructure insists that we pay attention to it because of its ability to overdetermine what is possible. The concept of *infrastructure* also forces us to understand the technological, cultural, social, and rhetorical as inseparable. Finally, there is the truly productive moment of broken infrastructures. Star and Ruhleder insist that infrastructures are most visible—and in some cases only visible—upon breakdown. I want to further insist that broken infrastructures are the most productive design moments. Broken infrastructures often reveal cultural disconnects if not conflicts ("whole" infrastructures can mask or suppress difference), and they often make explicit the underlying assumptions about possibility. This is one reason why the moments of intervention described in this chapter begin with broken infrastructures.

But what ideas should animate infrastructure design? One answer to this question must concern epistemological diversity because the problem of who knows (and the nature of that knowledge) is inseparable from a consideration of who can be persuasive. For this epistemological focus, I turn to the Greek concept of *metis*, which I introduced toward the end of the fourth chapter. Detienne and Vernant (1978) understand *metis* as a type of intelligence:

> There is no doubt that metis is a type of intelligence and of thought, a way of knowing; it implies a complex but very coherent body of mental attributes and intellectual behaviour which combine flair, wisdom, forethought, subtlety of mind, deception, resourcefulness, vigilance, opportunism, various skills, and experience acquired over the years. It is applied to situations which are transient, shifting, disconcerting and ambiguous, situations which do not lend themselves to precise measurement, exact calculation or rigorous logic. (pp. 3-4)

Detienne and Vernant—and later Atwill (1998) and Johnson (1998)—understand *metis* as enabling the less powerful or capable of reversing relations and practices of power. It is a way of knowing that makes available ways of acting. Indeed, for each of the theorists here, the only way to defeat a more powerful adversary is through *metis*. That is, the only hope those less powerful have of defeating those more powerful is by possessing ways of knowing—*actionable* ways of knowing—that enable reversal. To put it even more strongly, the less powerful must develop a *metis* if they hope to have any chance of success (for Atwill and Johnson, *metis* is a form of knowledge that forms part of the *techne* of rhetoric).

As an animating feature of infrastructure design, the usefulness of *metis* is more clear in the work of James Scott (1998). Scott's book, *Seeing Like a State*, is an examination of how the modern state gradually came to understand its people and environment to make easier and more rational common state functions like taxation or planning. One result was a simplification of complex human and natural systems that resulted in what Scott calls "maps," which enabled the state to actually remake human and natural worlds. And this is precisely what the modern state has done. Scott develops four elements that are present in the state-driven "fiascos" of the 20th century (e.g., mass collectivization of farming): administrative ordering of nature and society, high-modernist ideology, the authoritarian state, and a prostate civil society. Central to all elements is a theory of knowledge that ignores practical knowledge, local and informal processes, and inventiveness. Toward the end of his book, Scott turns to the issue of what to do about any design initiative inattentive to local knowledge or *metis*. Scott identifies four "small lessons" that might drive design decisions:

1. *Take small steps*: Given contingency and ignorance as starting places, prefer to move in small steps and to move slowly.
2. *Favor reversibility*: Do interventions that can be undone.
3. *Plan on surprises*: Accommodate the unforeseen and the unexpected; that is, create plans that allow this.
4. *Plan on human inventiveness*: Assume that people, sooner and later, will have better ideas and therefore should be able to change plans. (p. 345)

To Scott's own lessons, I draw two others from his work:

5. *Plan for/with concrete subjects*: Scott makes the point that the subject of modernist planning was always abstract: "the citizen," "the working class." This enables the violence, often unintended, that Scott describes and moral philosophy warns of (e.g., Benhabib, 1992, 2004; Habermas, 1993; Young, 2000). The modernist reduction of humans and the natural world to their "most basic," "essential," or "quantifiable" element is a necessary precondition of modernist planning. Situated and concrete design is a counter-impulse.[1]
6. *Create metis -friendly institutions*: As Scott writes, "An institution, social form, or enterprise that takes much of its shape from the evolving *metis* of the people engaged in it will thereby enhance their range of experience and skills . . . the quality of the institution and its product depends on engaging the enthusiastic participation of its people. . . . In the case of housing, for example, its success cannot be severed from the opinions of its users" (p. 356)

Scott's measure of a good institution is simple: does the institution enhance the capabilities of its people or hinder them? Stated differently, does the institution allow people to better their lives on their own terms or prevent that productivity? *Metis* as a concept matters precisely because knowledge is central to the ability to write for community change. Atwill (1998), in particular, is clear on this point. For her, rhetoric is transgressive; it enables transformation to the extent that it facilitates the ability to invent in ways that are resourceful, clever, and surprising. I came to a similar place in a much more mundane way. Sitting in meeting rooms listening to "experts" and "nonexperts" spar, it became clear to me that to be persuasive, "nonexperts" needed more than moral authority or vague citizen rights. They (we!) needed to come to an explicit understanding of their own expertise and become persuasive in terms that expert institutions would recognize. That is, "nonexpert" communities are required to work in ways recognizable to expert institutions but in ways that are "resourceful" and surprising.

I began to see my own usefulness, then, in terms of how I—and "we" in terms of the writing programs and research center with which I am affiliated—could help make explicit the rhetorical burdens of the less powerful. If we think of this in terms of infrastructure, we might ask: does an infrastructure support the creation of new, local knowledge? Does it enable and reward small steps, changes in course, and the interactions of real people and communities? Does a given infrastructure, in other words, support invention?

THE UBIQUITOUS PUBLIC MEETING

There is no more common rhetorical situation in community life than the meeting. The ability to perform well in a meeting—even if that performance means listening attentively and quietly—is a valuable skill and certainly part of any contemporary art of rhetoric. If we think of meetings as a genre, and I think we should, then there are certain subtypes of meetings that are common—predictable even—in community life. One is certainly the organizational meeting—what we might think of as an internal genre— a meeting within an organization. Another is the meeting of a deliberative body, such as a town council meeting, and this is a meeting with its own complex sets of rules and literacies. But the most important genre of meeting is the "public meeting," what McComas (2003) understands to be "among the most common and traditional methods of public participation in the United States" (p. 164; see also Simmons, forthcoming, for an in-depth discussion of the public meeting and public deliberation; and Throgmorton, 1996). I have spent many hours in public meetings, and citizens writing to change their communities must feel as if they have spent a good share of their lives in them. I opened this chapter with a snippet from a public meeting. Here I want to deepen my discussion of the public meeting as a key rhetorical situation, focusing on the meeting as infrastructure. More to the point, I want to discuss how Stuart Blythe and I, through our work with people in Harbor, worked to design the public meeting as a type of infrastructure that would support invention.

Katherine McComas (2003), who has written perhaps the best article on the public meeting as a commonplace communication situation, captures nicely the ideals framing the use of the public meeting in the United States:

> Firmly rooted in democratic traditions, public meetings symbolize certain American rights of free speech and assembly, where citizens gather and express their views openly and freely about their government. Public meetings also manifest democratic notions of political equality and popular sovereignty, referring to the equal right among citizens to exert influence over political actions, as well as the belief that, since government derives its authority from citizens, it must respond to the needs of its citizenry. (p. 164)

McComas notes as well that there are sound pragmatic reasons for taking public meetings seriously and valuing what comes from them: decision-making processes can be more just, sound, and widely accepted (see Simmons, forthcoming). However, and as clearly illustrated in the opening to this chapter, public meetings are fraught with problems. Handled badly, they can exacerbate problems. When manipulated, they do violence to participatory processes and relatively powerless communities.

McComas notes that the form of public meetings can vary from the informal to the formal, although, as I discuss later, I have seen little difference in how meetings are conducted in terms of "formality." McComas cites Heberlein's (1976) taxonomy of informative (delivery of information), co-optative (allowing citizens to "let off steam"), ritualistic (merely satisfying legal requirements to hold meetings), and interactive meetings as a useful way to think about the range of public meetings. Like McComas, I believe that Heberlein's categories are as useful today as they were 30 years ago. I would go further to say that most public meetings blend these four purposes in varying combinations, depending on the needs of those sponsoring and often "delivering" the meeting.

The public meeting, as McComas describes it in her study and as I have experienced it, is generally a presentation on a technical issue by a recognized expert (30-60 minutes in length) followed by questions and answers (another 30-60 + minutes). On the surface, a simple rhetorical situation. As a genre, the meeting is more complex. As an infrastructure, it is more complex still. Simply put, the public meeting is a highly standardized forum deeply shaped by the institutional practices of government bodies (that often sponsor them) and expert institutions that often supply the expertise. The meeting is fundamentally a report, delivered often by means of multiple media—voice, print documents, PowerPoint, charts and graphs—that would be normal within expert institutions. That is, the audience for this book would immediately recognize the rhetorical performance of the public meeting as nearly identical with an academic presentation. The performance of the audience is similarly shaped by these standards and related, but invisible, values and expectations. The audience is expected to ask technically appropriate and relevant questions of the expert. They are not expected to ask questions that are off-topic, loud, or offensive. They are certainly not expected to stand on their chairs and scream at the expert, although I have seen that happen often enough. There is much that could be written about the meeting as a complex and often confused rhetorical situation. There are audience problems woven throughout the situation, and this mismatch between speaker and audience expectations can explain a great deal of the failure that many people experience in public meetings.[2]

In our work in Harbor, however, we had more pressing needs. We knew that there was a history of awful public meetings. The meeting-as-report with which I opened this chapter was perceived by those with whom we worked in Harbor as both normal and ineffective. Even interactive public meetings went very badly in Harbor. The most important story I heard regarding "interactive" public meetings in Harbor is the following: In an effort to promote dialogue, interactivity, and improve community relations, the U.S. Army Corps and EPA organized an interactive public meeting at a community center in Harbor. The meeting was organized around discussion tables, and at each table, there were individuals from an expert institution and a poster or display of the science of the Harbor project. It was literally a "textbook" structure for a public meeting to foster high levels of public engagement and good will. The public reaction was not textbook. People felt that they were getting different stories from different experts and that the modular structure of the meeting was designed to "divide and conquer" the community. The meeting was stopped after a representative from a community environmental group and a city official (one male, the other female) had to be separated for fear that their shouting match would turn physically violent. The failure of this type of public meeting placed considerable pressure on TOSC to come up with something different.

As representatives of TOSC, we knew that we needed to do much better with TOSC's public meetings. Unlike others, however, we understood the problem of the public meeting differently. We saw the problem with the public-meeting-as-report as a problem of invention. Namely, the ways that public meetings are typically conducted do not support the invention practices of citizens. Think about it. Imagine yourself in a room receiving an oral report on the technical and scientific issues associated with a plume of contaminated groundwater flowing or sitting under your community. Could you ask intelligible questions at that moment in time? More to the point, if you had more time to digest the report and do some research, would you be better prepared? I hope so. This was our goal, to create via the public meeting an infrastructure that supported citizen invention in Harbor.

Our first task in reinventing the infrastructure of the community meeting in Harbor was to create conceptual and temporal space between the report and the meeting. The meeting for which we were preparing was one about the characterization of the sediments in the canal that was to be dredged. "Characterization" in this case means how well the scientists understand the biochemical composition of the sediments, and based on this understanding, what the best scenario is for handling the sediments. In a pattern that is typical for a TOSC project, TOSC hired a sediment expert to review the scientific work of the U.S. Army Corps of Engineers. The TOSC report, and thus the reason for the meeting, was to report the results of this technical review.

Our principal strategy for separating the report from the meeting was rather simple: we would distribute the report document a few weeks before the meeting. As simple as this might sound, such a strategy is rather disruptive. For our project manager at TOSC, the idea was both attractive yet *different*. We had to be sure that this process wouldn't be too disruptive for the sediment expert TOSC was flying in for the meeting. There was also the concern that in distributing the report beforehand, those in the community inclined to protest either TOSC or the results would have ample time to get organized. Organized protest was a concern for TOSC because it is disruptive to TOSC's educational mission. From my point of view, of course, organized protest at the TOSC meeting would be a sign that the strategy had worked—*any* sign of prepared, coordinated activity was precisely what the strategy was designed to foster. TOSC ultimately agreed to this change in practice.

Our impulse to separate the report from the meeting was based on evidence collected in the community. As I wrote in chapter 4, we had focused our attention on how people in Harbor understood and communicated their understanding of the dredging project. We knew, therefore, that there were effective networks for distributing print documents, both in their original and with an attached summary. In some cases, we knew that people would only see a summary.[3] We also knew that the summaries produced by Barbara's group would not simply summarize the TOSC document but would also likely include some fact checking and other forms of inquiry. In distributing the report weeks before the meeting, we wanted to support these inventional practices.

In terms of the meeting structure itself, we still began the meeting with an oral report from the TOSC sediment expert, but instead of a full oral report, which would have lasted at least forty-five minutes, we asked the expert to keep to a strict fifteen minute précis of the report. The goal was to move quickly to questions from the community and devote much of the meeting time to this purpose. The result was a meeting that was in many ways effective. We received a number of anecdotal reports that the meeting was good, even the best ever associated with the project.[4] But from my observations, the meeting was simply normal: folks asked some really good questions, some even referring to the report document; folks asked some challenging questions and called into question TOSC's independence; people asked some questions that seemed, to me, an outsider, off topic; and some gave speeches and performed in other ways that are expected in public meetings. In many ways, then, normal.

Yet, we achieved something infrastructurally different with this public meeting. As I attempt to illustrate in Figure 5.1, the traditional public meeting is based on a familiar communication model. What is important about this communication model is not its linearity, which is the focus of so many critiques of similar models. What is essentially wrong with this model is its erasure of the space (and time) for invention. In altering how we deployed the institution of the public meeting, we attempted to enable that space and time, but not in any paternalistic or directly supportive way. We simply gave people the time to do what we knew they would do—invent their own understandings of the report. The benefits for TOSC were considerable. The structure meant that the report distributed before the meeting was not the "final" report; thus, its conclusions were potentially reversible. We also opened up our meeting processes to surprise, and, of course, the inventiveness and expertise of and from individuals and organizations in Harbor. I don't want to idealize this intervention. At the same time, however, I don't want to minimize the potentially transformative possibility of new infrastructures. In this case, our attempt to enable a writing process that constituted a new form of social interaction in Harbor could be powerful indeed, if it were to become invisible, sunk into the very nature of things.

GRASSROOTS

Earlier in the book I described the Capital Area Community Information project and its goals of investigating both the usability and usefulness of

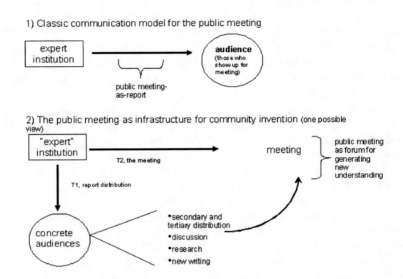

Fig. 5.1. Conceptual comparison of public meeting infrastructures

the CACVoices website and to create new tools with people in the Lansing area that support their work. These new tools include the core website architecture itself. As I have reported in this book, we have made some progress with the project in terms of usability. At this point in the project (December, 2005), we are in the process of completing a redesign of the CACVoices website to test if we have solved the critical usability problems. We will then move to observations of individuals and organizations in context to see how the new site supports their work.

As I have also made clear throughout this book, one of the specific tools that has captured my imagination for some time is the publicly accessible database. I see these databases as a metaphor for the development of networked computer functionality in general. That is, I understand these databases as one example of the more general phenomena of the migration of "expert" technologies to "nonexpert" users. I have written about this dynamic elsewhere (Grabill, 2003a), but for my purposes here it is only necessary to understand this problem in terms of where and how new computer technologies are developed. As Schuler (1996, 1997) has long noted, nearly all new technologies are developed within predictable contexts that we might understand as "expert" in some way: development labs, university research projects, in response to business needs, and so on. In other words, most computing tools are developed as a response to specific problems as articulated by a user community, but that user community is almost never users in civic or community contexts. Yet, what happens with increasing speed and frequency is that these technologies migrate outside their contexts of designed use with no adaptation. Just as significant a variable in this migration is the well-intentioned use of computer networks to push tools toward communities. Those pushing these technologies would like to place technologies of power in the hands of those with relatively little power. I don't see this dynamic of expert technology migration changing. Nor would I want it to. These technologies are central to the inventional practices of those writing for community change, but their centrality is often more an impediment than a help.

The CACI project was designed to explore the dynamic I have outlined here. It was also designed to intervene in some way; the precise nature of that intervention and its impact has yet to be determined or measured. But here I would like to write about a piece of infrastructure that we are building currently, one that flows from the CACI project but that has taken on a life of its own.[5] We call this tool Grassroots, and it is an explicit attempt to support invention in communities.

Grassroots is a response to the inventional problems of existing CACVoices databases in at least two ways. First, it is an asset mapping tool, which means that users can map positives about a community, not just problems. Users thus have control over what they are mapping. Second, it is an attempt to build geographic information systems (GIS) interfaces that are easy, pleasant, and fun to use, and that also provide resources for persuasive arguments. Let me begin first with the issue of GIS tools and interfaces. One commonplace of publicly accessible databases is that the results of data queries are often returned in the form of maps. This is not always true, of course, and not all data can be easily represented geographically. Still, data maps are actually quite useful. This form of data representation is complex and, therefore, allows one visual display to represent layers of data. The geographic displays also allow people to easily visualize the relationships between particular indicators (e.g., crime) and their neighborhood. Additionally, the maps are fun to play with, an issue that I take quite seriously as a design principle and that we discovered to be true in our usability evaluation.[6]

Although fun and potentially powerful, the database tools within CACVoices only allow users to map variables in existing databases. These databases were created and are maintained by government agencies interested in indicators that will drive their policymaking and service delivery

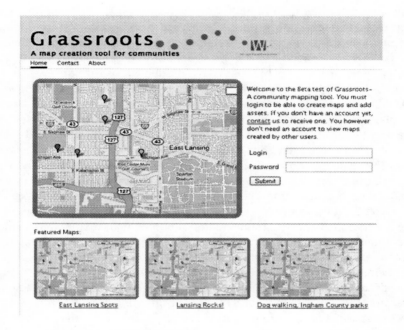

Fig. 5.2. Interface for Grassroots

decisions. Not surprisingly, then, these databases measure problems in communities: crime, sickness, and so on. But what if people in a community wanted equally powerful visual displays at their disposal to support an argument based on strengths in addition to—or opposed to—measurable weaknesses in a community? What tool might they use? These are the questions that we have been asking. Thus, Grassroots is an effort to provide people in communities with a robust tool that produces professional quality visualizations that are reusable for making arguments. Grassroots is also intended to solve usability problems; indeed, we want it to be fun to use (see Diehl, Grabill, Hart-Davidson, & Iyer, unpublished manuscript, for an elaboration of these issues).

Grassroots is writing software. It is really rather a simple tool in the genre of the "mashup." Grassroots is built onto Google Map's API.[7] Let me walk through a basic writing process using Grassroots. I'll locate the Allen Neighborhood Center in Lansing and its most recent initiative, the Hunter Park project. The Hunter Park project is the focus on a "Cool Cities" grant that ANC and other community partners won from the State of Michigan. The project is to create a paved perimeter path around the park and a greenhouse within the park. The path is to encourage exercise and use of the park as a recreational space. The greenhouse is part of ANC's food security program and will enable year-round production of vegetables and other plants. The greenhouse will then become part of ANC's neighborhood-based Community-Supported Agriculture (CSA) project, a youth garden scholars program, and other food-related events. Both the ANC itself and the Hunter Park project are significant neighborhood assets and worth locating, both physically and rhetorically.

The basic functionality of locating the center via an address is relatively easy to do (see Fig. 5.3). But as the figure shows, one feature of Google Maps, and thus of Grassroots, is the ability to create information bubbles that can be used to display text, links, images, and media. For the Allen Neighborhood Center, I simply created a bubble with textual information. For Hunter Park, I have created a bubble with image data (see Fig. 5-4). These maps can be information rich—much richer than the simple maps I have created here—but the issue that cannot be missed about these maps is that users are literally writing their own databases when they use Grassroots, databases that can persist over time and be used and added to by multiple users. It is one way to provide support for the coordinated knowledge work that takes place in communities.

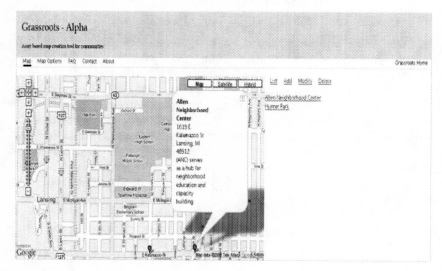

Fig. 5.3. Map of Allen Neighborhood Center with text data

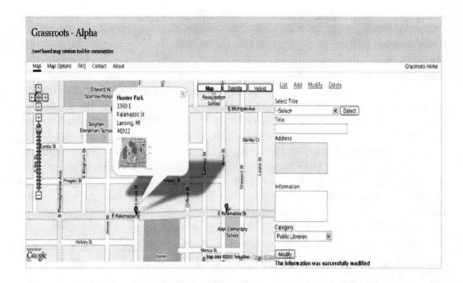

Fig. 5.4. Map of Hunter Park with image data

Grassroots constitutes a significant change in what is possible, both in terms of what organizations can write and how they can write. Given the way I have described the ICT-mediated inventional practices required of those writing for change in communities, the ability to write databases is important. Writing teachers and researchers may resist this notion, but it is clear to me that the database is something that citizens in the 21st century must learn to write. It is a part of the literacy toolbox. The start to a database that I created for the neighborhoods around Hunter Park contains a number of data points. These data points are not simply the information bubbles and what they contain, but also the interpretive possibilities of the GIS interface itself, which shows roads, parks, major institutions, and a number of spatial relationships and potential interpretations of these relationships. Furthermore, I can save my map. And in saving it, I can make this effort part of the coordinated work of an organization or a community. Others can add to it, delete from it, and so on. It is a database of things that we think are important.

Perhaps more powerful is the story that I can tell with Grassroots but not with any other database tool in Lansing. Given existing databases, I can map crime, low birth weight babies, and properties that have code violations attached to them. But I can't mark the greenhouse in Hunter Park, designate that part as the center of a "Cool Cities" project, or point out the beautiful yards, trees, activities, and people in this neighborhood. Given the coordinated collection of data and information, it is possible to massage that into new knowledge about that community. It is possible, even, to capture the wisdom of the experienced and make it persistent for current and future use. It is possible, in other words, to write persuasive documents because it is also possible to collect, manage, and maintain a database that serves as a resource, as the memory of past inventional work, as a commonplace book of ideas, arguments, and stories.

In addition, Grassroots is significant because it offers the possibility of dramatically changing the local information infrastructure itself. In chapter 4, I described the frustration of Allen Neighborhood Center's inability to share the knowledge they create. This is true for all organizations in the Lansing area, a failure that actually underlines the power of CEC's strategy of distributing copies of issue summaries to individuals and organizations in Harbor. Power is not only exercised by those institutions capable of making databases and effective use of advanced information technologies; power is also exercised by those institutions that can share that data. Those rhetors involved in the making *and* sharing of knowledge wield significant power in public life. They are obviously more capable of sharing their stories, but they are also more capable of determining the boundaries for the stories that others can tell. Just as significant is the ability to develop relationships based on the need for others to access the information and tools that powerful institutions use. Knowledge is power to the extent that it is used, shared, even given away. This is currently an exercise of power not available to many community organizations. Given the capacity of organizations to generate knowledge about their communities, can they make it persistent and available to others within their community or organization? Can they reuse it effectively? Can they make it available to others? *When* does a local information infrastructure emerge in a community? Only when a critical piece of infrastructure is created (or recognized) that allows people to transform the existing infrastructure into something new. In a sense, then, the power of Grassroots is that it exists. Such is the power of mundane things.

WRITING TEACHERS MAKING INFRASTRUCTURE
(a variation on the theme *WRITING TEACHERS WRITING SOFTWARE*)

Invention in the community

In the fourth chapter, my purpose was to show how I have observed invention taking place in communities. As part of that discussion, I glossed the discourse of expertise and the way in which "nonexperts" or "the public" are positioned by expert institutions. In mapping how groups write, I also showed the range of documents and the array of technologies required. I also tried to show where infrastructure was missing or broken and where the infrastructures currently available failed to support the writing required. In this chapter, I turned to making infrastructures as that essential and missing step. I intentionally used two very different examples to make this argument. The example from Harbor is, on the surface, more concerned with oral communication rather than written communication. It is also easy to see the Harbor example as nontechnological. Reading that example as somehow exclusively oral and atechnological would be wrong. In my effort to render visible the infrastructure that TOSC made, I do not want to make invisible the existing practices of invention and infrastructures in Harbor. What TOSC did does not make sense without what people in Harbor already were doing. Coordinated, technologically supported writing is the way work gets done in Harbor.

Grassroots is in many ways my answer to the problem of how to render the invisible visible. My answer for how those in relatively powerless communities recognize local knowledge—*metis*, even—in their midst and deploy it to good effect. This is a significant problem, of course, and not one I have solved here. But it is a problem that writing researchers are particularly well-positioned to solve because writing is an essential part of any infrastructure built to help local communities write persuasively. In the 1980s, writing teachers wrote software, and much of it was software designed to support invention. I have always thought that this impulse was one of the most creative and powerful reactions within the field of computers and writing to the problems of how to write powerfully with advanced information technologies. My colleagues and I at the WIDE Center find ourselves, in 2006, possessed by the same impulse. In the case of the projects described in this book, making infrastructures was a function of an action research strategy. In Harbor, the work that became meaningful to members of CEC was the development of a reporting strategy that was ethical and respectful. Here in Lansing, there are a number of action strategies, and all of them are related in some way to making new tools with people in communities to support their work. A second component of the action strategy of these projects is more conceptual and concerns an approach to research that accounts for the powerful as well as the marginal. I think I understand how the powerful invent and write, and furthermore, I think I understand the ways in which powerful institutions want their infrastructures designed to support what I have been calling *knowledge work*. What I have tried to show here is that the rhetorical practices of the less powerful constitute a similar form of knowledge work. My goal has been to be useful by making infrastructure to foster more effective use in communities. To continue this work, writing teachers might need to start writing software again.

NOTES

1. The concreteness of my own "subjects" is something that I wrestle with. In this book I have used concepts like "citizen" and "nonexpert" because they are convenient abstractions. They are poor representations for the people with whom I have worked in conducting the research that is represented in this book. What I take from Scott is the warning never to confuse concrete and abstract subjects or, worse yet, to elide the concrete with an abstraction.

2. Risk communication experts often focus on audience problems—(mis)perceptions of risk, lack of scientific literacy, and so on—as the reasons why public meetings so often go bad. EPA churns out guides for public participation that include material on running effective public meetings. TOSC is expert at it in many ways. I have seen nothing in either the scholarly or practical literature that focuses on the public meeting either as a genre or as a forum—as a rhetorical situation that can and should be understood as such.

3. We emailed the report to many individuals and organizations in Harbor; however, we also knew that print documents were important, and so we also mailed many copies of the document to key people in Harbor.

4. Our inquiry was not designed to compare meeting styles and therefore to measure "effectiveness" or some other response in the audience. See McComas (2003) for a look at what such a study design would look like.

5. This marks yet another shift in the "we" invoked in this book. Amy Diehl, the graduate student with whom I have worked on the CACI project, has taken a lead on this initiative, along with another graduate student, Vishal Iyer, who works for the Writing in Digital Environments (WIDE) Research Center here at Michigan State University. Bill Hart-Davidson and I are also involved in this effort; Grassroots is a project of the WIDE Center that is also connected and ultimately responsible to our partners in the Lansing community.

6. We evaluated the usability of two databases. One returned data in tables, the other as a map. Although our users failed to complete data queries using both tools, users spent considerably more time using the GIS database. The mean time for the GIS database was 5:57, with 30% of the users declaring that they had completed the task successfully. The mean time for the database that returned data tables was 2:32, with only 10% of the users reporting success. One clear reason given to us for the differences in time spent on task was that "playing" with the GIS database was fun.

7. Here is a somewhat more technical description of how it works. Google Maps can locate on a map any addressable location. Addressable in this case means a house or street number. This address corresponds to a geocode supplied by the United States Geological Service—another part of the Federal data system. In this way, the Google Maps API enables the interaction between a user and a SQL database of locations.

8. We are working on a new functionality for Grassroots that will allow users to "point and click" as a way of adding a location on a map. Hunter Park, after all, has no street address; neither would a beautiful tree that one may wish to note on a map of community assets. We are also working on the ability to draw lines on a map, which will allow users to map walking routes and other nondriving wayfinding.

6

WRITING PROGRAMS AND PUBLIC LIFE

As I write this, I am also preparing for a series of meetings in Lansing about the development of a community media center. Community media centers are variable in their design, but most of them provide support for public access television and new media content development. Others also provide community radio access. The one we are developing will include these features along with a writing center.

This initiative is perhaps the most "grassroots" project with which I have been involved. A loose group of people have come together in the last year around the idea that access to the tools to make and distribute media were lacking in Lansing and that meaningful community development depended on better access. Some in this group are existing public access television producers, both as individuals and as institutions. Others are public health professionals. Still others are members of neighborhood or other community development groups. My interest and involvement is layered. On the one hand, I am participating as a citizen. On the other hand, I cannot help but be interested in the project because of my work.

As part of my involvement, I have been paying attention to our work with local governments, the cable company, schools, community groups, and others to imagine, argue for, and hopefully make real this media center. To do this, we have really been involved in conceptualizing infrastructure at a level of abstraction and complexity that dwarfs my discussion of infrastructure in chapter five. I have also been attentive to the fact that we struggle as a group to coordinate our work meaningfully and write persuasively. In fact, as I write this, I am fearful that the project will fail precisely because we have failed to write persuasively.

Our writing problems are both significant and commonplace. Tonight I have been asked to attend a meeting in which we will discuss with whomever shows up the idea for the community media center. The goal is to get people excited about the idea. Tomorrow night I have been asked to attend a smaller meeting with a consultant working for a law firm examining the community media center idea for the City of Lansing. For the community media center to become real, the City must agree to work with us to develop the idea. Two significantly different meetings, purposes, and audiences. What we have needed all along is a project manager who could coordinate our work. But we really are a loose, ad hoc group of citizens, and nobody has the time to manage this project. As a result, we have no clear message, and the documents we have produced, especially our business plan, are not sufficient to be recognized by expert institutions as professional, particularly given the fact that we are asking for a substantial sum of money and the responsibility for managing public access to media. We have the capacity to be successful; we haven't been able to articulate that capacity.

My current problem is a type of writing situation that our students will confront over and over again. They will encounter it less so in school, unfortunately, because writing situations there are highly scripted and require little genuine invention. They will encounter similar intellectual problems as knowledge workers on the job. They will also have to be effective knowledge workers as citizens. And to coordinate this work, they will need to write in the ways I have understood writing in this book. How well do we prepare students for their lives as knowledge workers and writers? This is the question I take up in this chapter.

THE PURPOSES OF WRITING PROGRAMS

I joke with graduate students sometimes that regardless of the location, purpose, or intent of one's research in rhetoric and composition, the commonplace rhetorical move in writing about research must be an articulation of its relevance to the first-year writing classroom. I find this attachment to the classroom attractive for the way it ties the field to practice. It is, however, limiting for a research program. As a codirector of a research center in this field, I sometimes worry that some of our work may have a difficult time finding a home in one of the discipline's journals because so many of our projects are not directly concerned with the classroom. So I have often found myself resisting the impulse—and the pressure from reviewers—to return the results or implications of my work to the writing classroom. And then I feel guilty about it. Ironically, this last chapter was not originally planned to focus on teaching writing. Nor did my reviewers request it. Instead my work in communities has caused me to rethink the purpose, scope, and nature of writing programs. I share this thinking as a way to close the book.

A history of the modern university could be written with the history and purpose of writing instruction as a touchstone. Arguments about the purpose of writing instruction are often connected to arguments about the purpose of the university itself. My favorite articulation of this history comes from Sharon Crowley (1998), who encapsulates the history of the purpose of writing instruction in this way:

> to develop taste, to improve their grasp of formal and mechanical correctness, to become liberally educated, to prepare for jobs or professions, to develop their personalities, to become able citizens of a democracy, to become skilled communicators, to develop skill in textual analysis, to become critical thinkers, to establish their personal voices, to master the composing process, to master the composition of discourses used within academic disciplines, and to become oppositional critics of their culture. (p. 6)

Crowley writes that most of these purposes come from composition's proximity to literary studies, which is a persistent problem. Some purposes, she says, are really from noncomposition folks speaking for composition. And the last four, she insists, are articulated by compositionists themselves. How many of these purposes are operational in your writing program? Quite a few are alive and well in mine.

Computers and writing, for its part, has always slotted its work into the larger flow of composition studies (e.g., making inventional software when the composition was interested in invention or investigating the affordances of computers for revision). Most importantly, the computers and composition community paid attention to computers when colleagues in literary studies and even composition did not. As Hawisher, LeBlanc, Moran, and Selfe (1995) write, one reason for this was the fact that those outside the community—administrators, book publishers, policymakers, and the like—were certainly paying attention to information technologies. But we also paid attention because the computers and composition community felt that computer technologies would actually help writing teachers "move toward better, more just, and more equitable writing classrooms . . ." (p. 2).

It is tough to gauge the impact that computers and composition has had on the larger purposes of writing programs. To be sure, the use of computers to write is pervasive, much more so than the use of computers to teach writing. Consider my own university. As Doug Eyman (2005) has written recently, about 12% of first-year writing sections at Michigan State University are taught in computer environments, either full or part time. This compares badly to places like Georgia Southern and Illinois State, which report rates of 100%. In general, Michigan State University is near the bottom when compared to most U.S. universities. There are a number of infrastructural issues at MSU preventing the teaching of writing in environments where computers and networks are available.[1] Some are related to the differences between "labs" and "classrooms" on campus and the total number of computer-rich environments relative to the number of sections of writing we teach each year. Other infrastructural issues relate to the history and culture of the writing program, its relation to the humanities on campus and how it has been defined (often in opposition to science and technology), and the specific culture of technology within the writing program itself, which sees technology as a "content area" much like "history" or "radical thought" or "culture." At Michigan State, then, "technology" is still treated as a special topic, as an option. Taken together, these are likely the reasons we lag behind, as embarrassing as this is to admit. But my point is really much deeper. What would it mean to take writing technologies seriously, as integral to rhetorical practice? As so deeply integral to "writing" that writing programs were built around the understanding that information technologies are deeply and meaningfully infrastructural to the enterprise of teaching writing.

It is still common for noncompositionists to articulate the purpose of a writing program, and this will likely be the case at most institutions for some time. As Erika Lindemann wrote, "Freshman English offers guided practice in reading and writing the discourses of the academy and the professions. That is what our colleagues across the campus want it to do; that is what it should do if we are going to drag every first-year student through the requirement" (qtd. in Sirc, 2002, p. 8). Most first-year writing programs exist because the campus wants them to exist—on their terms—not because the value of the first-year writing course, for its own sake, is widely recognized. Geoff Sirc (2002) is one of the few to attempt an argument for the intrinsic value of composition. I want to move in that direction as well, but as will become clear, in ways much different from Sirc's notion of composition as a "happening." Still, I thank Geoff Sirc for his line of reasoning and for reminding me of what Peter Elbow wrote in 1991. To paraphrase: college is short, life is long. I agree. And so, in addition to taking technologies seriously, what would it mean for writing programs to be explicitly civic, public, in ways informed by what I have learned in communities?

There is a history of thinking about the public value and purposes of writing instruction, of course. Much of the history supports Crowley's argument regarding the close connection of writing instruction to the literary (or what Berlin, 1996, would call the poetic). The English department's understanding of the purpose of writing has dominated how the university has understood it, and so for the most part, writing has always been taught as a way to deliver some species of literary interpretation (see Berlin, 1987, pp. 65-71, for typical early- to mid-20th-century curricula). And although there is little in Berlin's (1987) history that would suggest that the purpose of first-year writing was ever commonly tied to citizenship, to the habits of mind and corresponding rhetorical practices that would enable individuals—and groups—to be persuasive in public space, there is some precedent. Berlin discusses Glenn Palmer's 1912 essay contrasting the Yale model of teaching writing to the elite with the goal of literary production and the Harvard model of widely cultivating "good language habits" to "train a class of Philistines prepared for the everyday needs of democracy . . ." (qtd in Berlin, 1987, p. 43). Berlin also devotes some attention to Fred Newton Scott's "rhetoric for a democracy," but other than its clear connections to Dewey's educational thought and opposition to the elitism of most approaches to writing instruction (Yale), the precise intellectual connections to the everyday needs of a democracy are not clear. Most significant is Berlin's treatment of the work of Warren Taylor and other progressive-era teachers of writing. These teachers brought social problems and local communities into classrooms. Taylor, in particular, insisted that one purpose of college was to produce students who "realize the value of education in political action" (qtd. in Berlin, 1987, p. 88).

It is at the present moment that the turn to the public has been most visible. Christian Weisser (2002) calls the move to public writing the most recent and significant movement within composition studies: "Many current writing courses—and the theoretical and pedagogical discussions concerning them—attempt to prepare students for citizenship in a democracy, for assuming their political and social responsibilities, and for lives as active participants in public life" (p. 3). The most useful aspect of Weisser's work is to tackle what, precisely, "public" means, noting that the meaning of "the public" is not stable, certainly not consistent, and thus must be used carefully in constructing a public pedagogy. Weisser writes that some "use the term 'public' as a metaphor for how we might envision what takes place in the classroom. A few compositionists use the term more literally, suggesting that discourse as it exists outside of the classroom is an important area of investigation" (p. 43). Fragmentation in the meaning of the public becomes the problem that Weisser spends much of his book wrestling with, but I think Weisser has captured the essential tension within composition studies with respect to public writing: is the classroom a public space—that is, is the classroom a microcosm of the larger society—or can "authentic" rhetorical experiences happen only outside the classroom?

I'm not sure this tension is all that important, nor is the tension itself a product of the more recent turn to public writing. As Bruce Horner (2000) argues, "the expressivist strategies of the late sixties and early seventies . . . attempted to combat the seemingly unreal, or false, nature of the writing students have ordinarily produced for the composition classroom, often denigrated as 'pseudo-writing' or 'bastard discourse'" (p. 53). Horner then goes on to argue that what he calls the "practical pedagogies" offered as a response to the expressivist critique "have students learn to produce writing that conforms to criteria ostensibly set by the corporate world or by academic disciplines. However, these also accept dominant reified definitions of what constitutes real writing, definitions by which student writing will again inevitably appear lacking" (p. 54). Horner goes on to discuss the false distinction between the real and the contrived, between real writing and practice writing. His point is that notions of the "real" or "authentic" and their opposites are constructions—arguments—and that writing in the classroom is not any less real than writing outside the classroom. Horner would readily agree that these arguments about what matters—about, at heart, the purpose and value of writing instruction—are significant arguments about value. Horner's argument is that the work of students in classrooms is real work, actual labor that produces artifacts, always in response to problems posed and audiences addressed. His point is that the debate about the value of writing instruction should not be decided based on a false notion of what is "real work." Thus, from Horner's point of view, the writing classroom is always already public.

I am attracted to Horner's argument about the work that students do in classrooms and his critique of the work done in schools as something less than "real." At the same time, I think Weisser is correct that there is a way in which public writing constitutes a new kind of argument for the purpose and value of writing instruction. My argument, in turn, begins here with the claim that students need to be understood as already citizens before they come to us and as citizens while they are with us. Accordingly, it is necessary to understand the writing required to be an effective citizen as work—as knowledge work—and teach the rhetoric necessary to do that work. As Horner would insist, students are working in the first-year writing classroom, not pretending to work or preparing to work later in a more authentic context. So what kinds of work are we giving students to do? What sorts of infrastructures are we providing them? And what is the relationship of this writing work with the other writing work they are doing in their lives?

THE WRITING WORK OF CITIZENS

Those who write in communities to create change coordinate their work among a number of actors in what I have been calling an infrastructure that supports knowledge work. Here I want to revisit what I think of as the most essential and conceptually rich of the composing practices I have observed. My goal is to use these ways of working as an argument for how we might work similarly with our students in the schools where most of us teach.

First is the issue of who invents and who writes in communities. As I asserted in the fourth chapter, to study rhetorical practice in contemporary forums is to study how groups of people and organizations write. Rhetorical practice is fundamentally a function of organizations, not individuals. In terms of rhetorical theory, this means, of course, that a little less time might be spent studying the rhetorical acts of individuals (e.g., great speeches) and a little more time studying how groups of individuals or organizations perform rhetorically. This is not to say that individual writers no longer matter. It is merely to say that coordinated and collaborative acts of writing are the more meaningful units of analysis. If true, my assertion here has clear pedagogical implications.

Second is the issue of how an organization reads and what is read in communities working for change. In the organizations I observed, reading practices, like writing, were distributed and part of the inventional process within organizations. Although the distributed nature of reading matters, it is the reading acts that might be most important to highlight. That is, how individuals read is useful to consider. Few readers deployed what we might think of as the "close reading" techniques that are still often taught in English Departments—and English may be the only place at a university where reading is taught, either implicitly or explicitly. Still, the ability to read a text closely is useful, but so is the ability to understand quickly the purpose of a text, like a technical report, which is a rhetorical way of understanding a document. Once understood, readers in community organizations would immediately skim to sections relevant to them, often setting aside much of the document. In other words, people in communities read similarly to how professional writing researchers understand the reading practices of individuals and teams in corporate organizations. Outside the professional and technical writing classroom, I'm not sure writing programs teach reading, and even in professional writing this approach to reading documents is generally taught indirectly, by way of a module on, for example, document design or how documents "do work" in organizations. Then, of course, there is the issue of what gets read in communities. It is often scientific or technical in nature, and that covers a wide terrain that would include the natural sciences and public policy and engineering and law.[2] How poorly our writing programs are positioned in English—with its devotion to literary and cultural texts (narrowly understood)—if we want to be relevant to the public lives of our students as citizens. Disciplinarity cripples our ability to be useful.

Third is the issue of what organizations write. One way to approach this is to look quite literally at the generic features of what organizations write: reports, databases, and the like. I would like to approach this somewhat differently and focus on what organizations writing for community change *do*. They propose, they report, they analyze, they organize, they market, they motivate. What matters, first, is the rhetorical activity. What matters then is understanding the genres that best carry that activity. In other words, there is no such thing as a report. People report, and they do so using the vehicle appropriate to the situation. Sometimes that is an oral presentation, sometimes a memo, sometimes a letter. The fundamental issue is that just as people in communities need to learn the rhetorical habits of mind I have described here, so do our students need to learn to think in these ways. And then people, in schools and in communities, need to be able to perform effectively within the appropriate generic conventions. Thus, we see people in communities giving oral presentations (supplemented by various display technologies); conducting meetings (planning, managing, listening, negotiating, speaking persuasively); regularly using electronic communication such as email, mail lists, websites, blogs and new media performances; and what we would understand to be professional and technical writing (reports, memos, letters, newsletters, fliers, issues/technical summaries, research notes), including the ability to manage projects. Rhetors must be good at coordinating complex work over time.

Finally, there is the presence of the technological infrastructure. The basic layer includes the computers, networks, interfaces, databases, chairs, pens, paper, and other technologies that support commonplace inventional and performative practices in communities. In a recent article on infrastructural support for writing, my colleagues, Dànielle DeVoss and Ellen

Cushman, and I (2005) argue that new media composing, in particular, simply cannot take place without an appropriate infrastructure. The concept of *infrastructure* we use in that article is roughly the one that I have used in this book, and in the article we show the various ways that infrastructure matters to writing and how writing can be enabled when an infrastructure is in place and disabled when it has broken down. One of the most important statements we made in that article, I think, is this:

> Some of these issues need the attention of teachers and of program administrators, but we would be miseducating student writers if we didn't teach them that these issues—that which we can too easily dismiss as "constraints"—are indeed deeply embedded in the decision-making processes of writing. If students are to be effective and critical new-media composers, they should be equipped with ways in which they can consider and push at practices and standards in strategic ways. (p. 16)

In other words, it is important that infrastructural issues be seen as much more than technical or administrative work. They must be made visible as part of the composing process, both for students and for people with whom we work in communities. Infrastructural awareness, then, is part of the intellectual context for all productive writing projects.

We wrote that article in an effort to argue for new infrastructures to support new media composing. But we were also conscious of the fact that writing programs have long struggled to provide what I hesitate to call a basic infrastructure for composing. Here again I think the usefulness and power of a writing program is hamstrung by its history of being buried in the discipline of English, as well as within the administrative structures of English departments, where the infrastructure to support writing, conceived of in its broadest sense, has always been lacking. But blaming English is an insufficient response. Computers and writing has always been one of the few communities within the humanities capable of making infrastructures to support writing. This activity has waned in recent years. But it must become an object of attention, a meaningful deliverable of our teaching and scholarly activity, particularly if writing programs want to support writing across the institutions of public life.

THE WRITING WORK OF STUDENTS

I think classrooms and schools are sufficient public spaces, but I would certainly not argue against writing classrooms that are engaged with communities. I often teach classes that involve community work or service learning. What matters for me is the nature of the work we give students to do in the writing classroom, how we support that work, and most importantly, the *learning* that can and should take place as a function of engaging in that work.

First, however, I need to explain why the "public space" debate in composition, as usefully articulated by Christian Weisser, is an important but in my view insufficient approach to how we might think about the purpose of writing programs in terms of our students lives as citizens. Earlier I used Horner to interrogate the school-public distinction and the values often attached to that separation. I will return to Horner's critique. For now, however, I want to pose an alternative way to think about the civic spaces where our students write, or will write, very soon. Whereas Weisser's approach to this question is Habermasian, and therefore fundamentally historical, my approach is more empirical and rhetorical. Let me begin by recalling Figure 3.1, the representation of community in Harbor that I presented in the third chapter. That figure, and the way of thinking about public space that it represents, is important for my argument here.

The problem that this figure helps me ponder is that of the distinction between the *idea* of public space and actually existing forums. Locating the civic, as I prefer to think of it, is a difficult task for a number of reasons and cannot escape the multiple intellectual traditions and terms that Weisser also wrestles with: public space, public sphere, civic/civil society (and space), and civic culture. It is important to engage these terms and concepts because locating civic rhetoric conceptually is essential to locating it pragmatically. That is, in order to understand where contemporary civic rhetorical practice takes place, who engages in practices of invention and certain performances, and who (and what) constitute the audience, we must have some way of sifting through how we understand civic space and public life. My understanding of these terms moves through concepts of "civil society" and "civic culture" in order to develop a way to locate civic rhetorical performances.

Rhetorical training as a part of civic education and practice has ancient Greek and Roman roots, of course, and these traditions are still very much alive in how we conceptualize rhetorics of public life today (see

Hauser, 1999, pp. 14-24, for a brief overview; Farrell, 1993). Hauser notes that for both the Greeks and the Romans, there was little need (or opportunity) to conceptualize a public sphere outside the assembly. In different ways, organized political institutions were the location of public debate. Hauser goes on to trace the economic, political, and moral reasons for the development of the concept of civil society, which he defines as "a network of associations independent of the state whose members, through social interactions that balance conflict and consensus, seek to regulate themselves in ways consistent with a valuation of difference" (p. 21). Iris Marion Young (2000) also separates "civil society" from the state and separates it further from the economy due to the asymmetrical power relations between them. Peter Dahlgren (2000), for his part, would have us make an additional—and I think necessary—distinction between society and culture. He inserts the concept of a "civic culture," which is "anchored in everyday life and its horizons. Civic culture both reflects and makes possible a larger democratic system, while at the same time it is dependent upon the system for its institutional guarantees and parameters" (p. 335).

What do we have, then, that is distinct from the idealized notion of public space available from Habermas? What we have is a set of distinctions that are rhetorically and pragmatically important (and necessary to teach to students). We might usefully draw distinctions between the institutions of the state and a parallel notion of civil society, which, at least in Hauser's terms, we must understand as a network of nonstate institutions and organizations (from Young we get a notion of civil society that is more neo-Habermasian). I am also attracted to Dahlgren's further identification of a civic culture that makes possible democratic practices within a range of deliberative institutions. That is, a civic culture must exist to make available to individuals and groups certain values, ideologies, and ways of acting. The actual forums where deliberations take place, then, are those made available by the interactions between and among the institutions of the state and civil society and supported by a given civic and rhetorical culture. Any given forum is highly structured—fixed by participating institutions and their rules—and highly variable (e.g., supported by more fluid civic cultures and rhetorical norms). It is the forum as network, as rhetorical infrastructure.

I am suggesting that abstract notions of the "civic" are marginally useful, just as abstractions of the public are marginally useful. Indeed, Hauser concerns himself with the problems of monolithic constructions of "the public." He writes that "'*the* public' is a generic reference to a body of disinterested members of a society or polity and is no more informative to an understanding of social knowledge and social action than an undefined ref-

erence to 'they'" (p. 32).[3] Furthermore, he writes, these unhelpful general-
izations about the public fail "to capture the activities of the working part
of society engaged in creating cultural awareness, social knowledge, and
public policies and in evaluating deeds. These activities are often local, are
often in venues other than institutional forums, are always issue specific,
and seldom involve the entire populace" (p. 32). Like Hauser, I am ultimately less interested in the generic and more interested in the particular
forums of civic rhetorical practice—and in developing methods for locating
who or what "the community" is in a given situation. As I have suggested,
much contemporary theorizing about the nature of the public and the civic
either remains conceptually abstract or focuses on commonly recognizable
public forums: legislatures, political and cultural action groups, newspapers,
public speeches by recognizable rhetors, and other discursive forums (e.g.,
mass media analyses).

My interest is in those forums in which citizens—often nonexperts
with respect to either subject matter or communication—must speak,
write, or otherwise perform in the face of significant complexity and the
presence of recognized expertise. These forums are not discrete places but
nodes in a complex network of public spaces. This brings me, finally, back
to my diagram of "the community" in chapter 3 (Fig. 3.1). It is not possible to see concepts like "civic culture" in a figure like this, but it is possible
to see a fragment of the type of networked, actually existing forums where
deliberation takes place. Visible in that figure are the institutions of civil
society and the state. The waterway management board for the city of
Harbor convenes many of the meetings where deliberation happens. The
lines of connection and communication suggest other ongoing communicative moments: the sharing of issue summaries, meetings, phone calls,
and the like. And there are many moments, of course, when representatives of many of these institutions or organizations come together to perform "the civic," to enact the democracy that they have in Harbor.

In other places, I have turned to the practice of planning for a way to
describe my understanding of public forums (Grabill, 2003b).[4] Planning is
an *activity* that takes place in every community, in governmental and quasi-
governmental bodies, task forces, working groups, neighborhood associations, and so on. It is yet another example of a way to locate forums. I think
it is essential to work with students on what concepts like "civic culture"
and "civil society" mean in terms of their supportive role for rhetorical
practice. But just as important is helping students to map the institutional
networks that structure deliberative practice. If we look outside the schools
where we teach, we can work with students to map the communities
around the school. But a more accurate map would resist clean distinctions

between town and gown because, as a matter of civic rhetorical practice, clean divisions do not exist. Furthermore, this analytical work with students will reveal networks of a civil society within schools themselves. My university, which is one of the largest universities in the United States in terms of physical size and enrolls around 44,000 students each year, functions as a small city. Thus, for reasons different from those articulated by Horner (2000), I do not believe in clear classroom-community or university-real world distinctions. The people in our classrooms are citizens as well as students. We don't need to invent that identity for them. These same people, in ways we surely do not know, inhabit the institutions of civil society and participate in civic culture in ways we could not imagine for them. I don't believe that we need to take composition into public space in the way that typically means because our schools and classrooms are always already part of that network of civic institutions. The much trickier issue is providing students with meaningful opportunities to do the work of citizenship and to learn how to be powerful with that work.

Let me turn to that work, and in doing so, let me begin with the issue of student identity. I have asserted that our students are also "citizens" and many other things. Perhaps most centrally for my present purposes, they are not "experts" in the traditional sense of the term. As Berlin (1987) writes, "as beginning students encounter an overwhelming array of new ideas and new ways of thinking, the rhetorical training they bring with them inevitably proves—regardless of their intelligence or training—unequal to the task of dealing with their new intellectual experience" (p. 3). I think Berlin is correct with respect to rhetorical facility, but his assertion is also more generally useful. Our students are also a bit overwhelmed when asked to learn and work with new ideas and ways of thinking across the curriculum, but they also have considerable talent and expertise. The pedagogical trick, it seems to me, is helping students to develop inventional strategies that allow them to learn in the areas where learning must take place, and inventional strategies that allow them to mine what they already know, the expertise, or *metis*, from other lived and intellectual experiences.

What if a writing class were concerned with the problem articulated in the opening of this chapter? What if, in other words, the entire writing class were designed around making the public arguments necessary to advance an idea within a community? Of course, it also could be the major project in a class with other ongoing work, but the details don't matter much to me. My interest is in the *possibility* of structuring a writing class around a civic rhetoric that understands the kind of work involved in creating a community media center as commonplace knowledge work in communities.

Our students are capable of doing this work, and we are certainly capable of teaching and learning with them. A class of this kind would require real, ongoing projects in which students could play a role. Or cases modeled on typical work required to write for change in communities. It would require analytical work on the part of students to map communities, understand the institutions of public life, and develop conceptually and pragmatically appropriate models of the forums and civic culture of the contexts in which they are working.[5] And it would require us to teach and facilitate the inventional practices appropriate to do the knowledge work of proposing a community media center.

The expertise to teach knowledge work of this type is embedded in most if not all writing programs. To propose a community media center, students would need to conduct inquiries into the current state of media access in a given community, the state of media access in other communities, and do so from as many perspectives as possible. They will develop models for what might happen in their community, and based on those models, they will need to analyze the feasibility of them and perhaps choose one as clearly superior. Depending on how they choose to work, they might try to make this process more participatory—engaging as many people and ideas as part of the inventional process as possible—or they might choose to focus on generating interest and enthusiasm for an idea that they think is best. My point is that both decisions are choices about what "democracy" means and how decision making ought to take place in communities, and we should, of course, make those choices explicit for them.

They will need to manage their projects and so create alterative plans. They will need to schedule and conduct meetings, make decisions about work roles and work flow, and manage complex writing processes. They will produce many documents for multiple audiences, such as internal planning and analytical documents, and external documents in which they propose, report, cajole, organize, and persuade. They will invariably need to create a database to manage their information, and they will, of course, be pulling information from human and technological networks. They cannot do this work without advanced information technologies—who would or could teach this class in which the workspace of the classroom had only the technological affordances of desks, paper, chalkboards, and whatever cell phones and computers students brought with them? But we must help them learn how to leverage this potentially powerful information infrastructure. We should make it explicit for them, show them the connections, the benefits, and the threats to useful parts of the infrastructure and how they might contribute to it. There is no reason at all, in other words, why students could not also propose a community media center for the City of Lansing, Michigan, and there is equally no intellectual reason why writing teachers can't facilitate this work and learning. To make change in communities is hard work, and this is what that work looks like.

TOWARD A WRITING PROGRAM WITH A PUBLIC FACE

I closed the last section with an example of a project that a writing class might attempt. But what about a writing program? How might we think about a writing program such that work as described earlier could regularly take place, but much more importantly, how might we think of a writing program that could be useful to people in many institutional settings and throughout their lives? My colleague Lynée Gaillet and I took up this question in terms of our experiences at Georgia State University (Grabill & Gaillet, 2002). We wrote that the writing program at a metropolitan university, in particular, was called to be more than the administrative coordinator of a service course. We argued for moving toward a new model of the writing program that facilitated work across the university and within the community, a model for a writing program that also foregrounded "inquiry" as a primary value and activity. And we talked of ways to position the writing program to be the type of "community interface" that might facilitate meaningful and sustainable work for teachers and students and people working in community organizations.

For writing programs to be a meaningful part of public life, such institutional work is necessary. I have resisted writing about classrooms and assignments in detail because I am more interested in the forms of infrastructure that can be developed to support and encourage the work of students and teachers in schools. A theory of writing program design along the lines that Lynée and I started is essential. As long as writing programs are thought of as a service function of an English Department, then writing programs will be largely irrelevant to public life despite the best efforts of teachers, students, and programs. That model of institutionalization, with its long and unwieldy history, buries writing programs too deeply within institutional decision-making structures and encourages writing programs to look inward toward disciplinary models of work and not outward toward the meaningfulness of writing in how work gets done in the world. There has been much written on writing programs, institutional models, and the future of composition within or outside English studies. I do not wish to repeat that work here. It is simply important, I think, to make clear that the kind of teaching, learning, and working that I find meaningful in community life is largely incompatible with the existing institutional model of the writing program within English (understood either in disciplinary or administrative terms).

On a more positive note, two other impulses within the field of rhetoric and composition bode well for sustaining the kind of writing work with students that is necessary to help them be productive citizens in their communities. One is the emergence of writing majors and the continued evolution of strong WAC programs (where those exist). And the other is the idea, which I steal from my colleague Bill Hart-Davidson, that writing programs might usefully imagine themselves as providing support for life-long learning in writing.

The emergence of writing majors in particular promises a verticality in a writing program that has rarely existed. The writing major supports an intellectual depth that is necessary given the complexity of the knowledge work I have described in this book. Thomas Miller (2005) has written an extremely interesting survey of recent trends in rhetoric and writing majors, and his survey reveals a number of models, as well as his own critique of those models. My point is simply that the existence of a writing major on campus stands a good chance of both providing the curricular context necessary to teach the type of rhetoric I outline in this book and make that teaching, learning, and productivity visible within and outside the university. As for the writing program as infrastructure for life-long learning in writing, that is an idea that I leave for Bill to develop, although it may be the most compelling and radical program-related idea I have mentioned. Imagine a writing program, composed of a number of institutional nodes: a curricular initiative, a writing center with an internal and external face, a research center, and a global, largely virtual interface for supporting various models of online teaching and learning. We know that writing is difficult and that it is an art that one continues to learn throughout one's lifespan. We know as well that at times the learning demands are so significant that they require help—other students, teachers, and difficult-to-access moments of infrastructure. Our writing programs can become an essential part of the infrastructure of civic life within any number of communities. Some will need research-related support, others the drop-in pedagogies of a writing center, and still others courses or training. The writing program need not be a container that sends students and faculty into communities to study writing. Writing programs can be part of the very infrastructure that supports communities writing for change.

NOTES

1. My colleagues Danielle DeVoss and Bill Hart-Davidson have been leading our efforts to think about what we might call "the affordances of technological spaces" for teaching writing. In effect, they are moving us from computer classroom-based instruction to instruction in flexible spaces that include the ability to write with computes and on/with computer networks. Certain kinds of wireless spaces are a good example.

2. Let me address the issue here of teacher expertise with respect to the types of texts read. I understand that many of my colleagues, like me, have degrees from English departments and that many writing teachers like being in English and working with literary texts. Moreover, I understand the impulse to say that we cannot read material outside of our area of expertise because we are not, say, civil engineers or urban planners. But I am not suggesting that we read outside our areas of expertise as experts. I am suggesting that we read the discourse that is relevant to public life—however we define that—and that we become comfortable with the fact that when we do this, we are reading *with* our students, not as experts but as more experienced colleagues.

3. Charles Willard (1996) more skeptically and perhaps more usefully claims that "the public" is "largely an idea about American democracy. It is an entry point to a way of speaking about democratic life . . . a vehicle for idealizing democratic discourse, for describing a discourse space distinct from market and state and from private and technical discourses" (p. 11).

4. There is considerable work in the literatures of planning-related disciplines that describe planning, in various ways, as a form of rhetorical practice. The most significant example is perhaps Throgmorton's (1996) argument that "good planning is persuasive and constitutive storytelling about the future" (p. 5). For Patsy Healey (1996, 1997), the interpretive, communicative turn in planning is a move away from instrumental reason and the privileging of scientific knowledge. It is an attempt to understand "how people come to have the ways of thinking and ways of valuing that they do, and how policy development and policy implementation processes can be made more interactive" (1997, p. 28). The emphases of communicative planning, if practiced, mean that planners are less like cloistered intellectuals and more like facilitators, community organizers, and master communicators. For John Forester (1993), who perhaps more than anyone else has been responsible for introducing critical communicative theory into planning (using Habermas), one way to understand planning practices is by studying the organizational and institutional contexts in which people make meaning about values, priorities, and possibilities and therefore help shape physical and civic space (p. 4).

5. The default thinking here is to focus on communities "outside" school institutions, but this need not be the case. Schools have these forums, cultures, and decision-making processes as well.

REFERENCES

Agre, Philip E. (1995). Institutional circuitry: Thinking about the forms and uses of information. *Information Technology and Libraries, 14*, 225-230.

Ambite, Jose L., Arens, Yigal, Hovy, Eduard, Philpot, Andrew, Gravano, Luis, Hatzivassiloglou, Vasileios, & Klavans, Judith. (2001). Simplifying data access: The energy data collection project. *IEEE Computer, 34*(2), 47-54.

Ars Portalis Project. (2000). *Community networking gets interesting: A synthesis of issues, findings, and recommendations.* Retrieved October 23, 2000 from http://www.arsportalis.org

Asen, Robert. (2002). Imagining in the public sphere. *Philosophy and Rhetoric, 35*, 345-367.

Asen, Robert, & Brouwer, Daniel C. (Eds.). (2001). *Counterpublics and the state.* Albany: State University of New York Press.

Atwill, Janet. (1998). *Rhetoric reclaimed: Aristotle and the liberal arts tradition.* Ithaca: Cornell University Press.

Bazerman, Charles. (1988). *Shaping written knowledge: The genre and activity of the experimental article in science.* Madison: University of Wisconsin Press.

BBC World Service. (2001). *Climate change in the Canadian arctic.* Retrieved December 21, 2005 from http://www.bbc.co.uk/worldservice/sci_tech/highlights/010510_canadianarctic.shtml

Beamish, Anne. (1995). *Communities on-line: Community-based computer networks* (Masters thesis, Massachusetts Institute of Technology). Retrieved from http://sap.mit.edu/anneb/cn-thesis/

Beamish, Anne. (1999). Approaches to community computing: Bringing technology to low-income groups. In Donald A. Schön, Bish Sanyal, & William J. Mitchell (Eds.), *High technology and low-income communities: Prospects for the positive use of advanced information technology* (pp. 349-369). Cambridge, MA: MIT Press.

Becker, Howard S. (1982). *Art worlds.* Berkeley: University of California Press.

Becker, Shirley A. (2004a). A study of web usability for older adults seeking online health resources. *ACM Transactions on Computer-Human Interaction, 11*, 387-406.

Becker, Shirley A. (2004b). E-government visual accessibility for older adult users. *Social Science Computer Review, 22*(1), 11-23.

Benhabib, Seyla. (1992). *Situating the self: Gender, community and postmodernism in contemporary ethics.* New York: Routledge.

Benhabib, Seyla. (2004). *The rights of others: Aliens, residents, and citizens.* Cambridge: Cambridge University Press.

Berlin, James. (1987). *Rhetoric and reality: Writing instruction in American colleges, 1900-1985.* Carbondale: Southern Illinois University Press.

Berlin, James. (1996). *Rhetorics, poetics, and cultures: Refiguring college English studies.* Urbana, IL: National Council of Teachers of English.

Besser, Howard. (2001). The next digital divides. *Teaching to change LA.* Retrieved March 28, 2003 from http://www.tcla.gseis.ucla.edu/divide/politics/besser.html

Blyler, Nancy. (1998). Taking the political turn: The critical perspective and research in professional communication. *Technical Communication Quarterly, 7,* 33-52.

Borgida, Eugene, Sullivan, John L., Oxendine, Alina, Jackson, Melinda S., Riedel, Eric, & Gangl, Amy. (2002). Civic culture meets the digital divide: The role of community electronic networks. *Journal of Social Issues, 58,* 125-141.

Bousquet, Marc. (2003). The "informal economy" of the information university. *Works and Days, 21*(1&2), 21-49.

Bowker, Geoffery, & Star, Susan Leigh. (1998). Building information infrastructures for social worlds—The role of classifications and standards. In Toru Ishida (Ed.), *Community computing and support systems: Social interaction in networked communities* (pp. 231-248). Berlin: Springer.

Bowker, Geoffery, & Star, Susan Leigh. (1999). *Sorting things out: Classification and its consequences.* Cambridge, MA: The MIT Press.

Boyd, Clark. (2005). Hi-tech DIY to solve local problems. *BBC News.* Retrieved December 21, 2005 from http://news.bbc.co.uk/2/hi/technology/4276180.stm

Brandt, Deborah. (2001). *Literacy in American lives.* Cambridge: Cambridge University Press.

Brown, John Seely, & Duguid, Paul. (2000). *The social life of information.* Boston: The Harvard Business School Press.

Brown, Richard Harvey. (1998). *Toward a democratic science: Scientific narration and civic communication.* New Haven: Yale University Press.

Bryant, Donald. (1965). Rhetoric: Its function and scope. In Maurice Natanson & Henry Johnstone (Eds.), *Philosophy, rhetoric, and argumentation* (pp. 32-62). University Park, PA: Penn State University Press.

Cintron, Ralph. (2002). The timidities of ethnography: A response to Bruce Horner. *JAC: Journal of Advanced Composition, 22,* 934-943.

Corey, Kenneth E. (2000). Electronic space: Creating cyber communities in southeast Asia. In Mark I. Wilson & Kenneth E. Corey (Eds.), *Information tectonics: Space, place and technology in an electronic age* (pp. 135-164). Chichester, England: Wiley.

Crabtree, Brad, Chopyak, Jill, & Cobb, Clifford. (May 1999). *The great data paradox— Threats to the integrity of the federal data system in the "Information Age."*

Retrieved August 15, 2005 from http://www.redefiningprogress.org/ publications/pdf/datawatch.pdf

Craig, William J., Harris, Trevor M., & Weiner, Daniel. (Eds.). (2002). *Community participation and geographic information systems.* London: Taylor and Francis.

Crowley, Sharon. (1998). *Composition in the university: Historical and polemical essays.* Pittsburgh: University of Pittsburgh Press.

Dahlgren, Peter. (2000). The internet and the democratization of civic culture. *Political Communication, 17,* 335-340

Davenport, Thomas H., & Prusak, Laurence. (1998). *Working knowledge: How organizations manage what they know.* Boston: Harvard Business School Press.

deCindio, Fiorella. (2000). Community networks for reinventing citizenship and democracy. In M. Gurstein (Ed.), *Community informatics: Enabling communities with information and communications technologies* (pp. 213-231). Hershey, PA: Idea Group.

Denison, Tom, Johanson, Graeme, Stillman, Larry, & Schauder, Don. (2003). *Theory, practice, social capital, and information and communications technologies in Australia.* Retrieved May 3, 2006 from http://www.ccnr.net/?q = node/50

Detienne, Marcel, & Vernant, Jean-Pierre. (1978). *Cunning intelligence in Greek culture and society.* Atlantic Heights, NJ: Humanities Press.

DeVoss, Danielle, Cushman, Ellen, & Grabill, Jeffrey T. (2005). Infrastructure and composing. The when of new-media writing. *College Composition and Communication, 57,* 14-44.

Diehl, Amy, Grabill, Jeffrey T., Hart-Davidson, William, & Iyer, Vishal. (unpublished). *Grassroots: Supporting the knowledge of everyday life.*

Dominick, Jay, Hughes, Anthony, Marchionini, Gary, Shearer, Tim, Su, Chang, & Zhang, Juliang. (2003). *Portal Help: Helping People Help Themselves through Animated Demos.* UNC-Chapel Hill School of Information and Library Science Technical Report TR-2003-01. Retrieved May 3, 2006 from http://sils.unc.edu/research/publications/reports/TR-2003-01.pdf

Elbow, Peter. (1991). Reflections on academic discourse: How it relates to freshman and colleagues. *College English, 53,* 135-155.

Eldred, Janet Carey, & Mortensen, Peter. (1998). Female civic rhetoric in early America. *College English, 60,* 173-188.

Engeström, Yrjö. (1990). *Learning, working and imagining.* Helsinki: Oriente-Konsultit Oy.

Esterling, Kevin, Lazer, David M. J., & Neblo, Michael. (2004). *Home (page) style: Determinates of the quality of house members' websites.* 2004 National Conference on Digital Government Research. May 2004. Retrieved April 10, 2005, from http://dgrc.org/dgo2004/disc/presentations/itadoption/esterling.pdf

Eyman, Doug. (2005). *A report on technology resources for writing at Michigan State University.* Unpublished manuscript.

Farrell, Thomas B. (1993). *Norms of rhetorical culture.* New Haven: Yale University Press.

Feather, John. (1998). *The information society: A study of continuity and change* (2nd ed.). London: Library Association Publishing

Ferreira, Joseph. Jr. (1999). Information technologies that change relationships between low-income communities and the public, and nonprofit agencies that serve them. In D. A. Schön, B. Sanyal, & W. J. Mitchell (Eds.), *High technology and low-income communities: Prospects for the positive use of advanced information technology* (pp. 163-190). Cambridge, MA: The MIT Press.

Fidel, Raya. (1994). User-centered indexing. *Journal of the American Society for Information Science, 45,* 572-576.

Fischer, Frank. (2000) *Citizens, experts, and the environment: The politics of local knowledge.* Durham: Duke University Press.

Fischoff, Baruch, Watson, Stephen R., & Hope, Chris. (1984). Defining risk. *Policy Sciences, 17,* 123-139.

Forester, John. (1993). *Critical theory, public policy, and planning practice.* Albany: State University of New York Press.

Gaventa, John. (1993). The powerful, the powerless, and the experts: Knowledge struggles in an information age. In Peter Park, Mary Brydon-Miller, Budd Hall, & Ted Jackson (Eds.), *Voices of change: Participatory research in the United States and Canada* (pp. 21-40). Westport, CT: Bergin & Garvey.

Geisler, Cheryl. (1994). *Academic literacy and the nature of expertise: Reading, writing, and knowing in academic philosophy.* Hillsdale, NJ: Erlbaum.

Gellman, Robert. (1995). Twin evils: Government copyright and copyright-like controls over government information. *Syracuse Law Review, 45,* 999-1072.

Ghose, Rhina. (2001) Use of information technology for community empowerment: Transforming geographic information systems into community information systems. *Transactions in GIS, 5,* 141–163.

Gibbs, David, Tanner, Keith, & Walker, Steve. (2000). Telematics, geography, and economic development: Can local initiatives provide a strategic response? In Mark I. Wilson & Kenneth E. Corey (Eds.), *Information tectonics: Space, place and technology in an electronic age* (pp. 219-234). Chichester, England: Wiley.

Gilyard, Keith. (1999). African American contributions to composition studies. *College Composition and Communication, 50,* 626-644.

Goddard, Steve, Harms, Sherri K., Reichenbach, Stephen E., Tadesse, Tsegaye, & Waltmam, William. J. (2003). Geospatial decision support for drought risk management. *Communications of the ACM, 46,* 35-37.

Goody, Jack. (1986). *The logic of writing and the organization of society.* Cambridge: Cambridge University Press.

Grabill, Jeffrey T. (1998). Utopic visions, the technopoor, and public access: Writing technologies in a community literacy program. *Computers and Composition, 15,* 297–316.

Grabill, Jeffrey T. (2003a). Community computing and citizen productivity. *Computers and Composition, 20,* 131-150.

Grabill, Jeffrey T. (2003b). The written city: Urban planning, computer networks, and civic literacies. In Bruce McComiskey & Cynthia Ryan (Eds.), *City comp:*

Identities, spaces, practices (pp. 128-140). Albany: State University of New York Press.

Grabill, Jeffrey T. (2006). The study of writing in the social factory: Methodology and rhetorical agency. In Blake Scott & Bernadette Longo (Eds.), *Cultural studies approaches to technical communication*. Albany: State University of New York Press.

Grabill, Jeffrey T., & Gaillet, Lynée Lewis. (2002). Writing program design in the metropolitan university: Toward constructing community partnerships. *Writing Program Administration: The Journal of the Council of Writing Program Administrators, 25*(3), 61-78.

Graff, Harvey, J. (1979). *The literacy myth: Literacy and social structure in the 19th century city*. London: Academic Press.

Graff, Harvey, J. (1988). The legacies of literacy. In E. R. Kintgen, B. M. Kroll, & M. Rose (Eds.), *Perspectives on literacy* (pp. 82-91). Carbondale: Southern Illinois University Press.

Gurstein, Michael. (2000). Introduction: Enabling community uses of information and communication technologies. In Michael Gurstein (Ed.), *Community informatics: Enabling communities with information and communications technologies* (pp. 1-31). Hershey, PA: Idea Group Publishing.

Gurstein, Michael. (2001). Community informatics, community networks and strategies for flexible networking. In Leigh Keeble & Brian D. Loader (Eds.), *Community informatics: Shaping computer-mediated social relations* (pp. 263-283). London: Routledge.

Gurstein, Michael. (2003). Effective use: A community informatics strategy beyond the digital divide. *First Monday*, 8.12 (December 2003). Retrieved June 27, 2004 from http://firstmonday.org/issues/issue8_12/gurstein/index.html

Habermas, Jürgen. (1993). *Moral consciousness and communicative action* (Christian Lenhardt & Shierry Weber Nicholsen, Trans.). Cambridge, MA: The MIT Press.

Harrison, Teresa M., & Zappen, James P. (2003). Methodological and theoretical frameworks for the design of community information systems. Journal of *Computer-Mediated Communication, 8*(3). Retrieved from http://www.ascusc.org/jcmc/vol8/issue3/harrison.html

Harrison, Carolyn, & Haklay, Mordechai. (2002). The potential of public participation geographic information systems in UK environmental planning: Appraisals by active publics. *Journal of Environmental Planning and Management, 45*(6), 841–863.

Hauser, Gerard A. (1999). *Vernacular voices : The rhetoric of publics and public spheres*. Columbia: University of South Carolina Press.

Hawisher, Gail E., LeBlanc, Paul, Moran, Charles, & Selfe, Cynthia L. (1995). *Computers and the teaching of writing in American higher education, 1979-1994: A history*. Greenwich, CT: Ablex

Healey, Patsy. (1996). Planning through debate: The communicative turn in planning theory. In Scott Campbell & Susan S. Fainstein (Eds.), *Readings in planning theory* (pp. 234-257). Cambridge, MA: Blackwell.

Healey, Patsy. (1997). *Collaborative planning: Shaping places in fragmented societies.* Vancouver: University of British Columbia Press.

Herndl, Carl G., & Nahrwold, Cynthia A. (2000). Research as social practice: A case study of research on technical and professional communication. *Written Communication, 17,* 258-296.

Horner, Bruce. (2000). *Terms of work for composition: A materialist critique.* Albany: State University of New York Press.

Irwin, Alan. (1995). *Citizen science: A study of people, expertise and sustainable development.* London: Routledge.

Janangelo, Joseph. (1991). Technopower and technoppression: Some abuses of power and control in computer-assisted writing environments. *Computers and Composition, 9,* 47–64.

Johnson, Robert. (1998). *User-centered technology: A rhetorical theory for computers and other mundane artifacts.* Albany: State University of New York Press.

Johnson-Eilola, Johndan. (2005). *Datacloud: Toward a new theory of online work.* Cresskill, NJ: Hampton Press.

Kingston, Richard. (2002). Web-based PPGIS in the United Kingdom. In W. J. Craig, T. M. Harris, & D. Weiner (Eds.), *Community participation and geographic information systems* (pp. 101-112). London: Taylor and Francis.

Kretzmann, John, & McKnight, John. (1992). *Building communities from the inside out: A parth toward finding and mobilizing a community's assets.* Evanston: Institute for Policy Research.

Krouk, Danny, Pitkin, Bill, & Richman, Neal. (2000). Internet-based neighborhood information systems: A comparative analysis. In Michael Gurstein (Ed.), *Community informatics: Enabling communities with information and communications technologies* (pp. 275-297). Hershey, PA: Idea Group Publishing.

Latour, Bruno, & Hermant, Emilie. (1998). *Paris ville invisible.* Paris: La Découverte-Les Empêcheurs de penser en rond.

Lauer, Janice. (2004). *Invention in rhetoric and composition.* West Lafayette, IN: Parlor Press.

Lave, Jean, & Wenger, Etienne. (1991) *Situated learning: Legitimate peripheral participation.* Cambridge: University of Cambridge Press.

Liu, Alan. (2004). *The laws of cool: Knowledge work and the culture of information.* Chicago: University of Chicago Press.

Loader, Brian D., Hague, Barry, & Eagle, Dave. (2000). *Community informatics: Enabling communities with information communications technologies* (pp. 81-102). Hershey, PA: Idea Group Publishing.

Manovich, Lev. (2001). *The language of new media.* Cambridge: MIT Press.

Marchionini, Gary, & Mu, Xiangming. (2003). User studies informing e-table interfaces. *Information Processing & Management, 39*(4), 561-579.

McComas, Katherine A. (2003). Citizen satisfaction with public meetings used for risk communication. *Journal of Applied Communication Research, 31,* 164-184.

McIver, William J., & Elmagarmid, Ahmed K. (Eds.). (2002). *Advances in digital government: Technology, human factors, and policy.* Boston: Kluwer Academic Publishers.

Merrifield, Juliet. (1993). Putting scientists in their place: Participatory research in environmental and occupational health. In Peter Park, Mary Brydon-Miller, Budd Hall, & Ted Jackson (Eds.), *Voices of change: Participatory research in the United States and Canada* (pp. 65-84). Westport, CT: Bergin & Garvey.

Mirel, Barbara. (1994). Debating nuclear energy: Theories of risk and purposes of communication. *Technical Communication Quarterly, 3*, 41-65.

Miller, Carolyn. (1985). Invention in technical and scientific discourse: A prospective survey. In Michael G. Moran & Debra Journet (Eds.), *Research in technical communication: A bibliographic sourcebook* (pp. 117-162). Westport, CT: Greenwood Press.

Miller, Thomas P. (2005). How rhetorical are English and communications majors? *Rhetoric Society Quarterly, 35*(1), 91-112.

Monteiro, Eric, Hanseth, Ole, & Halting, Morten. (1994). Developing information infrastructure: Standardization vs. flexibility. Working Paper 18 in *Science, Technology and Society*. University of Trondheim, Norway.

Moran, Charles. (1999). Access: The A word in technology studies. In Gail E. Hawisher & Cynthia L. Selfe (Eds.), *Passions, pedagogies, and 21st century technologies* (pp. 205-220). Logan: University of Utah Press.

Mosco, Vincent, & Wasko, Janet (Eds.). (1988). *The political economy of information.* Madison: University of Wisconsin Press.

Ray, Ruth, & Barton, Ellen. (1998). Farther afield: Rethinking the contributions of research. In C. Farris & C. Anson (Eds.), *Under construction: Working at the intersections of composition theory, research, and practice* (p. xx). Logan: Utah State University Press.

Regan, Alison. (1993). "Type normal like the rest of us": Writing, power, and homophobia in the networked composition classroom. *Computers and Composition, 10*, 11-26.

Regan, Alison E., & Zuern, John D. (2000). Community-service learning and computer-mediated advanced composition: The going to class, getting online, and giving back project. *Computers and Composition, 17*, 177-195.

Rimmer, Peter J. (2000). Neighbours: Australian and Indonesian telecommunications connections. In Mark I. Wilson & Kenneth E. Corey (Eds.), *Information tectonics: Space, place and technology in an electronic age* (pp. 165-198). Chichester, England: Wiley.

Rohan, Liz. (2003). Reveal codes: A new lens for examining and historicizing the work of secretaries. *Computers and Composition, 20*, 237-253.

Rowan, Katherine. (1994a). What risk communicators need to know: An agenda for research. In Brant Burleson (Ed.), *Communication yearbook* (pp. 300-319). New Brunswick, NJ: International Communication Association.

Rowan, Katherine. (1994b). The technical and democratic approaches to risk situations: Their appeal, limitations, and rhetorical alternative. *Argumentation, 8*, 391-409.

Sandman, Peter. (1990). Getting to maybe: Some communications aspects of sitting hazardous waste facilities. In Thomas Glickman & Michael Gough (Eds.), *Readings in risk* (pp. 223-231). Washington, DC: Resources for the Future.

Sanyal, Bish, & Schön, Donald A. (1999). Information technology and urban pover-
    ty: The role of public policy. In Donald A. Schön, Bish Sanyal, & William J.
    Mitchell (Eds.), *High technology and low-income communities: Prospects for the
    positive use of advanced information technology* (pp. 371-394). Cambridge,
    MA: The MIT Press.
Schafft, Kai A., & Greenwood, Davydd J. (2003). Promises and dilemmas of partic-
    ipation: Action research, search conference methodology, and community
    development. *Journal of the Community Development Society, 34*(1), 18-35.
Scott, James C. (1998). *Seeing like a state: How certain schemes to improve the human
    condition have failed*. New Haven: Yale University Press.
Schön, Donald A., Sanyal, Bish, & Mitchell, William J. (Eds.). (1999). *High technolo-
    gy and low-income communities: Prospects for the positive use of advanced
    information technology.* Cambridge, MA: The MIT Press.
Schiller, Dan. (1988). How to think about information. In Vincent Mosco & Janet
    Wasko (Eds.), *The political economy of information* (pp. 27-43). Madison:
    University of Wisconsin Press.
Schuler, Douglas. (1996). *New community networks: Wired for change.* Reading, MA:
    Addison-Wesley.
Schuler, Douglas. (1997). Community networks: Building a new participatory medi-
    um. In Philip E. Agre & Douglas Schuler (Eds.), *Reinventing technology, redis-
    covering community: Critical explorations of computing as a social practice* (pp.
    191-218). Greenwich, CT: Ablex.
Scott, James. (1998). *Seeing like a state: How certain schemes to improve the human
    condition have failed.* New Haven: Yale University Press.
Selfe, Cynthia L. (1999). *Technology and literacy in the twenty-first century: The
    importance of paying attention.* Carbondale: Southern Illinois University Press.
Selfe, Cynthia L., & Selfe, Richard J., Jr. (1994). The politics of the interface: Power
    and its exercise in electronic contact zones. *College Composition and
    Communication, 45*, 480–505.
Sellen, Abigail J., & Harper, Richard H.R. (2001). *The myth of the paperless office.*
    Cambridge: The MIT Press.
Shannon, Claude E., & Weaver, Warren. (1964). *Mathematical theory of communica-
    tion.* Urbana: University of Illinois Press..
Shaw, Alan, & Shaw, Michelle. (1999). Social power through community networks.
    In D. A. Schön, B. Sanyal, & W. J. Mitchell (Eds.), *High technology and low-
    income communities: Prospects for the positive use of advanced information
    technology* (pp. 315-335). Cambridge, MA: The MIT Press.
Sillitoe, Paul. (1998). The development of indigenous knowledge: A new applied
    anthropology. *Current Anthropology, 39*, 223-252.
Simmons, Michele (forthcoming). *Participation and power: A rhetoric for civic dis-
    course in environmental policy.* Albany: State University of New York Press.
Simon, Herbert. (1969). *Sciences of the artificial.* Cambridge: The MIT Press.
Sirc, Geoffrey. (2002). *English composition as happening.* Logan: Utah State
    University Press.

Slack, Roger S. (2000). Community and technology: Social learning in CCIS. In Michael Gurstein (Ed.), *Community informatics: Enabling communities with information and communications technologies* (pp. 494-510). Hershey, PA: Idea Group Publishing.

Slovic, Paul. (1986). Informing and educating the public about risk. *Risk Analysis, 6*, 403-415.

Smith, R. S., & Massimo, C. (2003). Digital participation and access to geographic information: A case study of local government in the United Kingdom. *URISA Journal, 15*, 49-54.

Star, Susan L. (1996). From Hestia to home page: Feminism and the concept of home in cyberspace (pp. 30-46). In Nina Lykke & Rosi Braidotti (Eds.), *Between monsters, goddesses, and cyborgs: Feminist confrontations with science, medicine and cyberspace*. London: ZED Books.

Star, Susan L. (1999). The ethnography of infrastructure. *American Behavioral Scientist, 43*, 377-391.

Star Susan L., & Ruhleder, Karen. (1996). Steps toward an ecology of infrastructure: Design and access for large information spaces. *Information Systems Research, 7*(1), 111-134.

Stoecker, Randy R. (2005). Is community informatics good for communities? Questions confronting an emerging field. *The Journal of Community Informatics* [Online], *1*(3). Retrieved June 9, 2005 from http://www.ci-journal.net/viewarticle.php?id = 14

Street, Brian V. (1984). *Literacy in theory and practice*. Cambridge: Cambridge University Press.

Sullivan, Patricia. (1986). *Rhetoric and the search for externally stored knowledge: Toward a computer age art of research*. Unpublished doctoral dissertation, Carnegie Mellon University, Pittsburgh, PA.

Takayoshi, Pamela. (2000). Complicated women: Examining methodologies for understanding the uses of technology. *Computers and Composition, 17*, 123-138.

Throgmorton, James A. (1996). *Planning as persuasive storytelling: The rhetorical construction of Chicago's electric future*. Chicago : University of Chicago Press.

Tulloch, David L., & Shapiro, Tamara. (2003). The intersection of data access and public participation: Impacting GIS users' success? *URISA Journal*. Retrieved May 4, 2006 from http://www.urisa.org/Journal/APANo2/Tulloch.pdf

United States General Accounting Office. (March 2001). *Information management: Electronic dissemination of government publications*. Report GAO-01-428.

van den Besselaar, Peter, & Beckers, Dennis. (1998). Demographics and sociographics of the Digital City. In Toru Ishida (Ed.), *Community computing and support systems: Social interaction in networked communities* (pp. 108-124). Berlin: Springer.

van Willigen, John, Rylko-Bauer, Barbara, & McElroy, Ann. (Eds.). (1989). *Making our research useful: Case studies in the utilization of anthropological knowledge*. Boulder: Westview.

Venturelli, Shalini. (forthcoming). *Dynamics of knowledge culture: Civil society, culture & ideas in the global information age.* New York: Oxford University Press.

Warner, Michael. (2002). *Publics and counterpublics.* New York: Zone Books.

Weisser, Christian R. (2002). *Moving beyond academic discourse: Composition studies and the public sphere.* Carbondale: Southern Illinois University Press.

Willard, Charles Arthur. (1996). *Liberalism and the problem of knowledge: A new rhetoric for modern democracy.* Chicago: The University of Chicago Press.

Wiener, Norbert. (1948) *Cybernetics, or control and communication in the animal and machine.* Cambridge: The MIT Press.

Wiener, Norbert. (1950). *The human use of human beings; cybernetics and society.* Boston: Houghton Mifflin.

Wurman, Richard Saul. (1989). *Information anxiety.* New York: Doubleday.

Young, Iris Marion. (2000). *Inclusion and democracy.* New York: Oxford University Press.

AUTHOR INDEX

A

Agre, P.E., 24, 25, 26, 27, 28, 39, 83, *127*
Ambite, J.L., 74(*n5*), *127*
Arens, Y., 74(*n5*), *127*
Ars Portalis Project, 10, 11, *127*
Asen, R., 3(*n2*), 13, *127*
Atwill, J., 16, 84, 92, 93, *127*

B

Barton, E., 47, *133*
Bazerman, C., 26, 70, *127*
BBC World Service, 1, *127*
Beamish, A., 10, 11, *127*
Becker, H.S., 29, *127*
Becker, S.A., 74(*n5*), *127*, *128*
Beckers, D., 37, *135*
Benhabib, S., 64, 93, *128*
Berlin, J., 113, 121, *128*
Besser, H., 12, *128*
Blyler, N., 44, *128*
Borgida, E., 37, *128*
Bousquet, M., 21, *128*

Bowker, G., 28. 30, 30(*n5*), 36, *128*
Boyd, C., 1, *128*
Brandt, D., 3, *128*
Brouwer, D.C., 3(*n2*), *127*
Brown, J.S., 23, 23(*n3*), 24, 25, *128*
Brown, R.H., 60, 61, *128*
Bryant, D., 14, *128*

C

Chopyak, J., 31, 33, 34, 35, 35(*n6*), *128-129*
Cintron, R., 4, 11, *128*
Cobb, C., 31, 33, 34, 35, 35(*n6*), *128-129*
Corey, K.E., 21, *128*
Crabtree, B., 31, 33, 34, 35, 35(*n5*), *128-129*
Craig, W.T., 74, *129*
Crowley, S., 111, 113, *129*
Cushman, E., 116, 117, *129*

D

Dahlgren, P., 13, 119, *129*
Davenport, T.H., 23, 25, *129*
Denison, T., 9, *129*